"Markus Watson is a pa
the neighborhoods whe
thinker who puts ideas
listener who loves to explore the possibilities for God's people to live together in the most healthy and joy-filled ways. This book is a road-map for a church to find new vibrancy, new life, new joy. I heartily recommend it."

—Tod Bolsinger, VP and Chief of Leadership Formation at Fuller Seminary, author of *Canoeing the Mountains: Leading into Uncharted Territory*

"There's a lot of material out there about how to be the church in ordinary life—in the neighborhood and one's places of vocation. What is still amazing about so many of these books is how they're driven by what Markus Watson calls 'thingification,' a word that goes straight to the point. Behind the drives to 'connect' lie anxieties about survival and relevance but also a lack of theological imagination about who God is and what it means to be God's people in the local. Here Markus guides you through some of the threads in current life that have produced thingification and shares with congregations how to be guided by the Spirit into a different space."

—Alan Roxburgh, author of *Joining God, Remaking Church, Changing the World: The New Shape of the Church in Our Time*

"There is no shortage of voices reminding us that the church in the West (especially the US) has lost its missional bearings. And while recognizing that we have a problem is a vital first step in addressing what ails us, we also need to start imagining what it is that we are to do next. With equal parts creativity and practicality, Markus Watson does exactly that. Watson draws on both his expertise as a cultural interpreter and his on-the-ground pastoral experience with his own community to offer real-world suggestions for how the people of God might embody their mission differently in light of our current post-secular context."

—Kutter Callaway, Associate Professor of Theology and Culture at Fuller Theological Seminary, author of *The Aesthetics of Atheism: Theology and Imagination in Contemporary Culture*

"The Church has done Kingdom things in Empire ways for centuries. We're beginning to discover that and we'll need all the help we can get to imagine the way back to doing Kingdom things in Kingdom ways. Markus Watson provides such a resource, walking us through practical and hopeful new (old?) ways of being the Church."

—Mandy Smith, pastor of University Christian Church, author of *The Vulnerable Pastor: How Human Limitations Empower Our Ministry*

"The work of God's people extends far beyond the walls of the church. This book is an excellent guide for helping congregations discover and then live into the work that God is doing in many places."

—Kurt Fredrickson, Associate Dean for the Doctor of Ministry and Continuing Education, co-author of *That Their Work Will Be a Joy: Understanding and Coping With the Challenges of Pastoral Ministry*

"Finally, a thoughtful guide to the hurried and harried pastor. Markus Watson offers hard-won insight and deep theological reflection rolled into practical ministry expressions for today's world."

—Geoff Hsu, Executive Director of *Flourish San Diego*

"Beginning with a robust articulation of God's mission, Markus Watson provides a wise, compelling, and tangible way for God's people to navigate these complex times. This book is both pastoral and visionary, hopeful and realistic. It's a joyful invitation to join God's work in the world."

—Jim Mullins, pastor of theological and vocational formation at Redemption Tempe, author of *The Symphony of Mission: Playing Your Part in God's Work in the World*

"Frequently churches and those of us in leadership get caught in habits that distort our sight, drive misplaced priorities, and distract us from God's initiatives. Watson brings his ministry experiences, scholarship resources, and generative imagination into the service of God's on-the-ground presence and beckoning. He shows how we can engage each other, our friends, our churches, and our neighbors, in discovering how God is perpetually at work redeeming all of life."

—Mark Lau Branson, Homer L. Goddard Professor of the Ministry of the Laity at Fuller Theological Seminary, author of *Memories, Hopes, and Conversations: Appreciative Inquiry, Missional Engagement, and Congregational Change*

"In his important new book, Markus Watson tackles tough questions about how church can be relevant in contemporary society. By pointing congregations to an approach that is both incarnational and transformational, he steers pastors and lay people toward a hopeful future.

This should be required reading for any leader longing to make a lasting difference in the lives of people!"

—Nate Landis, Founder and President of *Urban Youth Collaborative*, author of *God Wants His Kids Back*

"Markus Watson recognizes that *what was is not what needs to be* going forward for many churches. His call for the creation of Vocational Connection Groups is a fresh way for churches to engage their communities and to be the Light of Christ in them. We are not living in 'status quo' times and Watson's call to action is a game changer for local churches."

—Dwight Gibson, Chief Explorer with *The Exploration Group*, contributor on *For the Life of the World* video series

"Markus is hitting home for many church leaders and communities in this book. *Beyond Thingification* is a piece I wish I had when I first began my ministry. The fact of the matter is, many churches and church leaders get wrapped up in things that aren't necessarily what the Church was truly meant to be. Markus takes time to unwrap these ideas in a well thought out manner, that ultimately points us back to the shalom we should be striving and living for. I highly recommend this book for any and all who are looking to strengthen their church's ministry and mission for the glory of God."

—Bobby Benavides, pastor of New Community Elkins, author of *Made for More: A Journey of Discovery and Purpose*

"For pastors, this book will bring about the wonderful truth that their focus doesn't have to be on getting as many people in the pews as possible, but on bringing shalom to their churches and neighborhoods. For laypeople, this book will inspire them to know that even if they are not on staff, their vocations and family lives are ministries that are just as important as the traditional ministries in the church. Markus Watson does a wonderful job encouraging both staff and non-staffers alike to come together to do something truly beautiful in their communities."

—Kate Hurley, author of *Getting Naked Later: Making Sense of the Unexpected Single Life*

"*Beyond Thingification* is intriguing and informative, a great read for any church desiring to join the mission of God in their unique cultural context. Instead of trying to fix the church, Markus Watson inspires us to live as healing communities, deeply inhabiting the world with the love of Jesus. With stories and practical ideas for the vocation of God's people, this is a great guidebook for our day."

—Christiana Rice, author of *To Alter Your World: Partnering With God to Rebirth Our Communities*

BEYOND THINGIFICATION

MARKUS WATSON

Beyond Thingification: Helping Your Church Engage in God's Mission

Spiritual Life and Leadership
San Diego, CA
www.spirituallifeandleadership.com
www.markuswatson.com
markus@markuswatson.com

ISBN 978-1-0828-0536-3

Churches today feel lost because they no longer know how to do ministry in our ever-changing world. Spiritual Life and Leadership helps churches get clear on what God is up to in their communities so they can help their people participate in the healing of the world. For more information, visit www.spirituallifeandleadership.com.

CONTENTS

INTRODUCTION

Self-preservation.

Self-propagation.

I believe these two words capture the frame of mind of most churches in Western culture today.

Either your church is trying to stop declining—a kind of survival mentality. Do whatever you can to keep the doors of the church open. The problem is that when we are consumed with self-preservation, it is easy to miss the marvelous things God may be inviting us into.

Or your church is focused on growing—where success is defined by how many people show up on a Sunday morning. And many churches *are* growing. Many churches *do* look very successful. Many churches feel quite confident in the achievements of their ministries. If you look at the goals such churches set for themselves, they almost always consist of numbers--size of attendance, size of offering, number of people in small groups, number of people volunteering in ministries, and so forth. When the goals of a church are focused on self-propagation, however, it becomes quite possible to miss what God wants to do through our church beyond our growing numbers.

For almost nine years, I served as the senior pastor of a Presbyterian church in San Diego. A lot happened during that time. We grew. We declined. We welcomed young families. We served our local schools. We went on mission trips to Mexico. We cleaned up an ugly old alley behind our church.

And we cut the budget.

Every year.

It was so frustrating. And it was scary. Why? Because I knew that eventually we wouldn't be able to cut program budgets anymore. Eventually, we would have to cut my salary. Maybe I should have had more faith or maybe I should have been less selfish. But, listen, I'm just being honest—I didn't want my salary cut.

I was definitely in self-preservation mode.

One of my practices at that church was to walk around the sanctuary a few times each day. That makes me sound very spiritual, doesn't it? Well, don't think *too* highly of me—it was mostly because I was trying to get my 10,000 steps per day! I did, however, use that time of walking in the sanctuary to talk to God. Sometimes I would pray over certain pews and the people who normally sat there, or I'd pray generally over the various sections of the sanctuary. Sometimes I would thank God for the good things that were happening. And sometimes I would vent my frustration.

On one of those frustrating days, I complained to God about how we were going to have to cut the budget—again! In a moment of exasperation, I silently cried out, "Lord, would you please tell me how to get more people to show up?! And how can I get them to give more money?!"

And in the very next moment, I thought to myself, "Aargh! I hate thinking this way. This is not what I signed up for when I became a pastor!"

I wanted to do more than just stress out over attendance and budget. What I wanted was to see people's lives transformed. I wanted to see our community transformed. And more than anything, I wanted to participate with God to bring healing and wholeness into people's lives and into the world.

It is incredibly easy to get caught up in a self-preservation mentality. It's also easy to get sucked into the self-propagation mindset of church growth. They are really two sides of the same coin, aren't they?

It's almost instinctive. And it has very little to do with what kind of church you lead. If you are in a church plant, the focus is likely on growing your numbers, providing an excellent worship experience, and demonstrating how fruitful your church looks to others in your church-planting network. If you are in a large church, the need for self-preservation/self-propagation might express itself in terms of increasing and improving programs, the number of small groups and volunteers, the number of campuses your church has, and making sure you hire only the best staff (and firing them if they're not the best). If you are in an older mainline congregation, self-preservation tends to revolve around, well, doing whatever it takes to keep from having to permanently shut the doors.

We live in a world in which success is defined by these very things: how many people showed up, how many people got baptized, how many dollars people tithed, how many new members joined. It's hard not to get caught up in the numbers. Numbers can become a kind of idolatry.[1]

When I was in my twenties, I was the high school youth pastor in a large congregation in Southern California. Every week, we had to report our numbers at the youth staff meeting. How many kids were at youth group? How many came to our Bible studies? How many kids came to the laser tag event on Friday night? With how many kids did I do "contact ministry"?

So, I get it. I have felt—and often still feel—the pressure of needing to stop declining or keep growing.

In order to relieve that pressure, we believe we need to start ministries. So that's what we do. We start programs. We try to get people to show up for our ministries and programs. We try to get people to do a bunch of "church stuff." When they do show up, we feel successful and we feel like we've carried out God's will. When they don't show up, we feel like we've failed and we wonder if somehow we've let God down or failed to properly hear his call.

Something about all this feels very wrong, doesn't it? Is this really what leading a church is all about? It's got to be about more than getting people to do "church stuff," right?

And that's where part of the danger lies—we may start to believe that God only works through his people when they are doing "church stuff." When they are serving as an usher. When they are in the worship band. When they teach Sunday school. When they are a middle school youth leader. When they go on a mission trip.

But doing "church stuff" is not what accomplishes the mission of God—at least not by itself. Doing "church stuff" falls under the umbrella of self-preservation and self-propagation. Rather, when our people engage in their callings—in their jobs, in their neighborhoods, in their families, and, yes, sometimes even in their churches—that's when the mission of God is fulfilled.

So, then... How can God's people—the church—truly live out the mission of God? I'm convinced that it's not through more or better church programs, but through *all* of God's people living out their own unique callings. This involves flipping a lot of our assumptions and expectations upside down. We tend to operate as though God's mission is accomplished when the church invites people to participate in the church's programs. I believe, however, that the mission of God is lived out when ordinary followers of Jesus participate in what God is already doing as they live out their vocations. And what ordinary followers of Jesus need from their churches is support and affirmation for the work and ministry to which God has called them in their places of vocation.

I'm not suggesting that we need a different kind of church (i.e., non-institutional, post-denominational, or whatever adjective you want to use). What we need is a different way of *being church*. So, let me pose a few questions as we begin:

- How might churches affirm and embrace the ways God has called people in the church to serve God where they live, work, eat, sleep, and play?
- How can churches equip their people to participate with God in bringing healing and wholeness—*shalom*—to the world around them through their various callings?
- Is it really possible that the mission of God will be fulfilled not by church programs, but through

the people of God as they live out their various callings?

- Is it possible, as a local church, to discover what God is up to in our neighborhoods and then participate with what God is already doing—beyond the walls of our churches—in the spheres of our people's vocations?

This book is for church leaders—especially those who are familiar with the question, "How can I get more people to show up and give more money?" but who also know that this is definitely not the right question. It's for pastors, for youth pastors, for worship leaders, for elders, for deacons, and for anyone else who has a leadership role in the church. It's for church leaders who are struggling to survive in a world for which they were not prepared in their seminary and ministry training. It's for those who are planting churches and want to begin right from the start with a deep sense of God's calling in their community. It's for those who are in churches that look like they're doing great, but sense that somehow something is missing. This book is for those who know their church could be so much more—and is called by God to be so much more—but can't figure out how to *get there*.

"Getting there" feels like an enormous obstacle. Is there anything churches can intentionally do to help their people live into their callings so as to fully participate in the mission of God?

I believe there *is* a way for churches to "get there." I believe there is a way for the church to embrace and affirm the unique callings of all of God's people. I believe there is a way that churches can begin to move toward a model of ministry that helps people live lives of fruitful mission in all spheres of their lives. And I believe that there is a way for the church to discern how God is inviting us to join him far beyond merely doing bigger and better ministry. In the latter chapters of this book, I will show you a very practical way for churches to 1) *help their people* live into their vocations and participate in God's mission, and 2) *learn from their people* so that the whole congregation can participate with God's work in the world. I call this approach a *Vocational Connection Group.*

Before we get to that, however, I want to explore some ideas to help us think deeply about nurturing our people in their callings and discovering how God is already at work in the world beyond the church's strategies and programs. I want to begin by considering the church's mission and how the church has lost its mission. We'll look at what it means for each person to have their own sacred calling—a vocation. And we'll explore why it is so important to recognize that God is already at work in the world; God is ahead of the church in the realms of our people's vocations. Finally, as promised, we'll look at how to implement and execute a *Vocational Connection Group* in your church.

But right now, let's begin by considering the mission of the church.

PART I

THE CHURCH IN A POST-CHRISTENDOM WORLD

1

COFFEE, SMOG CHECKS, AND CHUCK E. CHEESE

(OR WHAT IS THE CHURCH'S MISSION?)

Author H. Jackson Brown, Jr. once said, "Talent without discipline is like an octopus on roller skates. There's plenty of movement, but you never know if it's going to be forward, backwards, or sideways."[1] I resonate with that statement because I have often felt that way as a pastor. There has been lots of movement in the churches I've served, but I'm not sure we had a ton of direction.

As the pastor of a church, there was a lot of pressure to *do* stuff. I often felt like I needed to make a show of all the stuff we were *doing*. Sometimes, God did amazing things through all of our service and the work we were doing. But sometimes, our work amounted to very little—not much spiritual formation, not much evangelism, not much healing for the world. Sometimes the stuff we were doing didn't really seem to accomplish anything.

But... Because we had *done* something, we were able to show a video or share a story or offer a tribute on Sunday morning and make people feel like we had accomplished important work for the kingdom of God.

The problem came down to this: We weren't really clear about our mission as a church. We weren't clear on *why* we existed as a church. We weren't clear on who we were meant to be as a church.

So, we have to ask: What *is* the church's mission?

Entire books have been written about the mission of the church. And there is a vast range of ideas as to what exactly the church's mission really is. Is the church's mission:

- evangelism?
- social justice?
- to grow the church?
- to provide for those who are in need?
- to glorify God through our worship?

I would argue that the answer to these questions is... Well, yes. All of these! All of these and more are part of the church's mission.

But these are only *part* of the church's mission. Why? Because they are only *part* of God's mission.

And what is God's mission?

Well, I can tell you that the mission of God is much bigger than any of those mentioned above—bigger than evangelism, than social justice, than church growth or serving those in need or making beautiful worship music. The mission of God is much farther reaching than any of these.

And, yet, the mission of God can be captured in a single word: *shalom*.

Shalom

Shalom *is* the mission of God.

You may know that shalom is the Hebrew word for "peace." "Peace" is a good English translation of shalom, but it's important to understand that shalom means so much more than "an absence of hostility"—although that's a part of it. Shalom also means more than "inner peace"—although that's also a part of it.

The root of shalom has to do with being intact or complete. It indicates a daily existence that is characterized by harmony with nature, harmony with others, harmony with oneself, and harmony with God. Shalom is "a state of wholeness...and security embracing both the physical and spiritual dimensions and relating not only to the individual, but also to entire communities and relationships among persons."[2]

A "Very Good" World

The early chapters of Genesis may not explicitly use the word "shalom," but they certainly paint a picture of shalom. In Genesis 1, we see a God who calmly and deliberately speaks the universe into existence. The world is birthed out of the waters of chaos as the hovering Spirit of God ushers in a new creation. As God speaks the words, "Let there be..." God repeatedly says about his creation, "It is good." And at the end of the sixth day—after God had finished all the work of creating—God looked at everything he had made and said, "It is *very* good!"

Genesis 1 is the story of God speaking creation into existence, a creation whose primary quality is shalom. It is the story of God breathing life into humanity, a humanity whose relationships with God, with each other, with the creation, and even with their inner selves are characterized by shalom.

In Genesis 2, we see the emergence of human beings as co-creators and co-laborers with God, bringing even more shalom into the world. We see human beings charged with the responsibility to work the land and take care of it and to name the animals. We see a deep union between God and human beings. God cares that the man is lonely and wants him to be happy (Genesis 2:18). There is harmony and vulnerability between the human beings themselves. "They felt no shame," the author of Genesis tells us (Genesis 2:25). They had nothing to hide and nothing to fear in their relationship with one another. Shalom was present also in the relationship between human beings and the world God had created. When God put human beings in the Garden he charged them to they take care of the Garden (Genesis 2:15). The world God had made provided all that the people needed and the people tended to the well-being of the Garden. Everywhere you looked, in every relationship, shalom was abundant.

A Broken World

But then we come to Genesis 3. This is the part of the story where shalom is broken. Human beings make a decision. They decide that they can determine for themselves what is right and what is wrong ("the knowledge of good and evil," Genesis 2:17). In so doing, shalom is destroyed. The union between God and human beings is lost as we hear God cry out, "Where are you?!" The humans themselves are now divided, blaming and shaming one another. Even the creation itself is now contaminated and broken in its relationship with human beings.

Shalom is established and then broken. That's what happens in Genesis 1-3.

Genesis 4 through Revelation 22—the rest of the Bible—is the story of God working through humanity to *restore* shalom in the world. It is about the culmination of all things coming together to finally become who and what God intended them to be.

That's shalom. That's what God longs for in the world. That's where all this is heading.

Tastes of Shalom

In the meantime, we get little tastes of shalom. We take small steps toward shalom. In the realms of relationships, health, economics, poverty alleviation, and so forth, we get to have little experiences of shalom that point us toward the final consummation of shalom in the new heavens and the new earth. Let me give you a few examples.

My wife, Robin, is really good with kids. She's also a fantastic leader. As the Director of Fletcher Hills Presbyterian Preschool,[3] she creates an environment in which both teachers and children can become their best selves. Children play, grow, draw, sing the alphabet, and learn about Jesus. Teachers get to use their gifts, skills, and love for children to participate in the shaping of these young lives to become healthy and whole adults. And parents can rest secure knowing their children are loved and well taken care of. All of these experiences—children having fun and learning, teachers living out their gifts as they bless children, parents resting secure knowing their children are safe—are all foretastes of the consummation of shalom to come.

After recovering from a severe head injury that he suffered while skiing, my friend, Dave, challenged himself to hike California's John Muir Trail. As he hiked, he fell in love with God's creation. Dave is a chef, and through this experience felt called to better love his neighbor—the earth—by preparing food in ways that are 100% sustainable and waste free. Now, whenever Dave caters parties and events, everything he uses to prepare and serve his meals are reused, recycled, and composted. He makes delicious food (Dave likes to call it "tasty-great!") that fosters community, celebration, and friendship. In the preparation, the eating, the table fellowship, and even the clean-up, there is a foretaste of God's coming shalom.[4]

My youngest son, Drew, is practically a shalom vending machine! Multiple times a day, out of the blue, Drew will say to me, "Daddy, I love you *sooo* much!" (In fact, he happened to say it just as I was typing that last sentence while sitting across the table from me at Starbucks, playing games on my phone!) If you're a parent, you know there's nothing quite like being told "I love you" by one of your kids. Why is it so wonderful to be told "I love you" by one of your children? Because it is a beautiful taste of the shalom that God longs for the whole world to experience.

I have two hobbies in which I experience foretastes of shalom in my life—surfing and movies. I'm not a very good surfer and I don't get into the water nearly enough. But I love the ocean. There is something of the divine in the sound of the waves, in the gentle rocking of my surfboard on the surface of the water, and there is a surrender to the ocean's power when I drop in on a wave. I get a small foretaste of the shalom to come when I surf; I also get a taste of shalom when I go to the movies. The joy of anticipation when the lights go down. Feeling the rumble of the bass in the theater's sound system. Sitting back as the credits roll at the end of a story well told. For me, that's an experience of shalom.

Speaking of movies (and TV shows), we love happy endings, don't we? Why? Because so often a happy ending paints a picture of restored shalom. I used to watch a show called *Falling Skies.* It's about a dad named Tom and his three sons as they try to survive in a world that has been invaded by aliens. Tom's youngest son, Matt, is ten or eleven years old and Tom doesn't want him carrying weapons or engaging the aliens. In one episode, Matt secretly goes "hunting" aliens with a friend. Tom is naturally upset about this and there's tension between them through the entire episode. After much drama (as you'd expect), the episode ends with both of them lying in their cots at the end of the day. But things aren't the way they should be. Father and son shouldn't be at odds with each other. Slowly, Matt gets up from his cot, walks over to his dad's cot, and looks down at him. Tom looks up at his son as the audience wonders what's about to happen. Tom then pulls back his blanket. Matt, who is really still a child, climbs into Tom's cot where he falls asleep in his dad's arms.

True confession: I cried when I watched that scene. In fact, I feel all choked up right now just thinking about it!

Why? Because it's such a beautiful picture of shalom—the restoration of a father-son relationship.

These are just a few examples. But the fact is, every time we see restoration, healing, and beauty, we are seeing shalom. We can catch glimpses of shalom everywhere:

- When a husband and wife reconnect after years of drifting apart, that's a step toward shalom.
- When a parent and child reunite after having been estranged, that's an experience of shalom.
- When two countries end hostilities, that's a manifestation of shalom.
- When a person's cancer goes into remission, that's a taste of shalom.
- When a person learns to embrace their past and live without shame, that's the beginnings of shalom.
- When a church feeds and clothes and houses the poor, that's a touch of shalom.
- When a person puts their faith in Jesus and enters into relationship with their Creator, that's a life-changing experience of shalom.

God wants the world to experience joy, hope, compassion, beauty, and delight. Why? Because God is a God of joy, hope, compassion, beauty, and delight. And these divine expressions of shalom can be experienced even in the seemingly mundane moments of life:

- When a person enjoys a cup of rich, delicious coffee, there is shalom in that cup of coffee.
- When a family has a super-fun day at the amusement park, that's an experience of shalom for that family.
- When your daughter lands a back-handspring, the delight of that moment is an experience of shalom.
- When a hiker jumps across a stream in the woods, there is shalom in that.

- When a person gets their car smog-checked so our air stays clean or begins to pay attention to what they can recycle or reuse, that's a move toward shalom for humanity and creation.
- When a single mom is able to pay her rent at the end of the month, that is a foretaste of shalom.
- And when she has enough left over to take her kids to Chuck E. Cheese, the joy they experience is the joy of shalom.

Shalom is so much more than an absence of hostility—the simple meaning of peace. Shalom has to do with a state of comprehensive well-being that touches every aspect of life. It is a kind of fullness of joy, of hope, of goodness, of justice, of health, of faithfulness, of compassion, and of love.

God's Mission

A world characterized by shalom is what God intended and what God longs for. It is why God called Abraham and his descendants, the people of Israel, to be a blessing to all the nations. It is why God sent his Son, Jesus, to live a life of shalom, to teach shalom, and make reconciliation—the restoration of shalom—between God and humanity possible. And it is why God continues to send his people, the church, into the world today—to restore shalom.

Restoration of Shalom

The restoration of shalom in all its fullness is the mission of the church because it is the mission of God. The church has been called to participate with God in bringing shalom to the world. The church's mission is to restore relationships between human beings and God, between human beings and each other, between human beings and God's creation, and even between human beings and themselves (an inner wholeness that God desires for people).

The beauty of this is that the mission of the church can take many forms. Perhaps your church focuses on:

- Meeting the needs of the urban poor.
- Meeting the needs of the rural poor.
- Providing safe places for people to heal who are struggling with addiction.
- Offering help to those with relational difficulties.
- Reaching out to those furthest from God with the life-changing news of redemption through Jesus.
- Providing environments where people can come and ask hard questions about faith.

One church's expression of God's mission may look different from another church's expression of God's mission. But both are being faithful to God and to the mission.

The first step to joining God's mission as a church is to recognize God's mission of shalom for the world and its place in that mission (against all the pressure to just get bigger and look successful!). The second step is to discern the unique way God is calling your church to join God in his mission.

Shalom For All

The goal of God's mission is the restoration of a world full of shalom. Shalom, as I mentioned, is a state of comprehensive well-being that touches every aspect of life.

Because God's mission is to bring full restoration and

healing to the whole world, God says some pretty outrageous things in the scriptures. I'm thinking, for instance, of Jeremiah 29:1-14.

Let me give you a little background. In 586 B.C., King Nebuchadnezzar conquered Jerusalem and took a huge portion of the population captive. These Israelite captives were carried away from their homes and resettled in and around Babylon. They had become strangers in a strange land who wanted nothing more than to go back home. No doubt many of the Israelite captives hated their Babylonian oppressors. They were afraid and needed hope.

Into this context comes the prophet Jeremiah with a message from God for the exiles living in Babylon. You would think God's message would go something like this: "Gather your weapons! Marshal your forces! Get ready to fight! Prepare to defeat your enemy and return to your home!"

But that's not the message God has for his people. God's message is this: "Build houses and settle down; plant gardens and eat what they produce. Marry and have sons and daughters..." (Jeremiah 29:5-6).

Not what they were expecting! But, wait. It gets worse.

The next thing God instructs his people to do—those who were living in exile under the thumb of a cruel oppressor—is to "seek the peace and prosperity of the city... because if it prospers, you too will prosper." Or, more markedly, "seek the *shalom* of the city...because if it experiences shalom, you too will experience shalom."

Outrageous, isn't it? God actually wants his people to pray for the welfare of their pagan captors!

Do you know what amazes me most about this? The thing that blows me away is that God desires shalom not only for the Israelites who worship God, but for the idol-worshiping Babylonians, as well. That's pretty incredible if you think about it! How will the Babylonians experience shalom? They will experience it when the people of God live out shalom by praying for their captors. We see something profound in this passage. We discover that God's goal is shalom not only for those who are his people, but also for those who are seemingly not his people.

Jesus demonstrates God's desire for *all* to experience shalom throughout his life and ministry. Over and over again, Jesus proclaimed not a gospel that was limited to a single group of people, but a gospel that was for *all*. Upon seeing the faith of the Roman centurion, for instance, Jesus says, "I say to you [those gathered] that many will come from the east and the west, and will take their places at the feast with Abraham, Isaac and Jacob in the kingdom of heaven" (Matthew 8:11). And in Luke 15, Jesus tells three parables—the lost sheep, the lost coin, and the lost son—to announce that shalom is not only for the religious, but also for "tax collectors and sinners" (Luke 15:1-32). It will not be only the people of Israel or only the "righteous" who will experience the shalom of God's great feast. Redemption through Jesus is available not only to those with good behavior or the right pedigree, but to the whole world!

After the death and resurrection of Jesus, we discover that God's longing for shalom extends even beyond human beings. The apostle Paul tells us that through Christ, God reconciled "to himself *all things*, whether things on earth or things in heaven, by making peace through his blood, shed on the cross" (Colossians 1:20, italics added).

Look at Paul's words again. What does God achieve through Christ's blood? Peace.

Paul writes this to a church in Greece using the Greek word for peace—*eirene*. But as a lifelong Jew and native

Hebrew speaker, Paul would surely have had in mind the Hebrew word—*shalom*.

Now notice for whom Paul says shalom is intended—"all things...things on earth...things in heaven." What is included in the shalom God longs for? Everything!

What is excluded from God's shalom? Nothing!

Is there anything in all creation, anything at all anywhere in the universe, about which God says, "I don't want you to experience shalom"? Not a chance!

The Trajectory of God's Mission

By now, I hope you can see the trajectory of God's mission. The mission of God is leading toward the restoration of all creation. We see the glorious fulfillment of God's plan at the end of Revelation. This is how the apostle John describes the ultimate realization of God's mission:

> Then I saw 'a new heaven and a new earth,' for the first heaven and the first earth had passed away, and there was no longer any sea. I saw the Holy City, the new Jerusalem, coming down out of heaven from God, prepared as a bride beautifully dressed for her husband. And I heard a loud voice from the throne saying, 'Look! God's dwelling place is now among the people, and he will dwell with them. They will be his people, and God himself will be with them and be their God. "He will wipe every tear from their eyes. There will be no more death" or mourning or crying or pain, for the old order of things has passed away (Revelation 21:1-4).

Isn't that a wonderful vision of the world? A world in which all things are as God intended them to be!

This is the mission of God. *This* is the mission Israel was called to fulfill (Genesis 12:3). *This* is the mission Jesus came to fulfill. Jesus came to restore shalom between God and humanity, between human beings and one another, between human beings and the created order, and even within people's inner lives. God is and always has been a shalom-bringer.

And *this* is the mission that you and I have been called to participate in. We have been called to join with God in restoring shalom to all creation in this broken and sin-scarred world.

I don't know about you, but when I think about this mission, I get so excited! How could I not want to be a part of that. Unfortunately, the church has often done a poor job of living into the call to participate in God's mission. This is true of the church today. We're not doing a particularly good job of bringing shalom into the world. Why? Well, it has to do with something called "Christendom," and it is to that topic that we turn in the next chapter.

2

FROM OUTCAST TO OVERSEER

(OR HOW THE CHURCH LOST ITS MISSION)

We live at the tail end of an era in Western civilization known as "Christendom." I've heard Christendom defined in essentially two ways. The first is that Christendom simply means Christianity. Christianity and Christendom, in this sense, are basically synonyms. The second definition says Christendom is that part of the world in which Christianity prevails—as a religion, as a philosophy, and as a way of life. In other words, when Christianity is at the center of culture and has great power within the culture—that's Christendom.

When I speak about Christendom in this book, it's this second definition that I have in mind. Yes, some folks think of Christendom as a synonym for Christianity, but the two are really quite different. Whereas Christendom refers to a cultural locus of power, Christianity refers to a faith-based lifestyle and a relationship with God through Jesus.

I want to take a look in this chapter at Christendom. I want to explore the origin of the era and culture that we call

Christendom and, more importantly, I want to unpack how Christendom has shaped the church as we know it today.

What Is Christendom?

In *Missional Church: A Vision for the Sending of the Church in North America*, Christendom is defined as the "centuries in which Western civilization considered itself formally and officially Christian."[1] Christendom was that period in history (about the last 1500 years) when the whole culture was essentially a Christian culture—a time when Christianity was at the center of power in Western culture. It was the historical era in which Christianity prevailed.

Where Everyone Is a Christian

Christendom was a time and a cultural context in which, if a person wanted to maintain a good reputation in the community, they had to attend church regularly—meaning every week! In his book, *Canoeing the Mountains*, Tod Bolsinger tells about a friend of his who said, "You know, when I began my ministry in a church in Alabama, I never worried about church growth or worship attendance or evangelism. Back then, *if a man didn't come to church on Sunday, his boss asked him about it at work on Monday.*"[2]

But what if you couldn't make it to church? What if you had to miss a week? How's this for a solution? "Robert Chambers, the Victorian Scottish publisher and naturalist," writes Leonard Sweet, "kept pews in two different churches. If he was absent from one, the congregation presumed he was in the other and his reputation remained intact."[3] In Christendom, people went to great lengths to maintain the appearance of faithful religious practice.

But, as you've probably already guessed, that's not the world we live in anymore. Very few places, if any, in Western society consider themselves to be "formally and officially Christian." And there is certainly no need to maintain a religious appearance in order to be well-respected. In fact, some might argue that the opposite is true in our world today!

Alan Kreider, in *The Change of Conversion and the Origin of Christendom*, says, "In Christendom everyone is a Christian."[4] Or, at least, everyone is considered to be a Christian. Everyone acts as though they are Christian and believes Christian things. As a result, in Christendom culture, when churches are planted they start to grow because church attendance is simply an expected social norm. You go to church—it's just what you do.[5]

Christendom Church-Planting

One of my former congregations was launched when the founding pastor went door to door through the streets of the community informing residents that a new Presbyterian church would soon be established. All he had to do was let people know when and where this new church would meet. And that was enough to virtually guarantee that the church would grow in attendance and membership.

Why?

Because it was 1953! And because back then those who had a Presbyterian background were certain to attend the new Presbyterian church. All the founding pastor had to do was find the Presbyterians who were moving into town.

In Christendom, going to church is just what you do.

That, however, is a far cry from the early church in the first 300 years of Christianity. People didn't just "go to church" in those days. Being a Christian involved deep commitment and great risk. The early church was at worst persecuted and at best marginalized by the Roman Empire.

So, how did the church of Jesus Christ go from being persecuted and marginalized to being the dominant cultural power in Europe? I'm glad you asked!

The Rise and Fall of Christendom

Even though the church had a lot of cultural power throughout most of its history—an era we call "Christendom"—it wasn't always that way. During the first 300 years after Jesus, the church had very little power at all in the culture, which at that time was dominated by the Roman Empire.

And yet, somehow, in the fourth century, the church ended up at the very center of power in Western society.

How did that happen?

How Did Christendom Begin?

The era we call Christendom is largely considered to have begun when the Roman emperor, Constantine, converted to Christianity in A.D. 312. Christianity was legalized the following year when Constantine issued the Edict of Milan, giving Christianity "a position of privileged equality with other religions."[6]

This changed everything for Christianity. Up until this time, the church had been in a position of near powerlessness in the Roman Empire.[7] But the moment Constantine announced his edict, the church was thrust into a position of cultural authority and the period of Christendom began.

The church found itself in a completely new situation. For the first time ever in its history, the church had political and cultural *power!* The church finally had a say in the halls of government. At last, the church had the opportunity to influence policy.

The question is, was that a good thing? Barry A. Harvey, in *Another City*, says this:

> "With the conversion of Constantine...the church faced a new situation for which it was largely unprepared. The same empire that had regularly ridiculed (and from time to time persecuted) the members of Christ's body was now expressing interest in their story of salvation and its criteria of true universality, even to the point of inviting the church to order the imperial household."[8]

Can you imagine experiencing such an incredible change of status? To go from outcast to overseer?

Now that the emperor himself claimed to be a Christian, Christianity was no longer a ridiculed and persecuted religion. Instead, it now held a place of great advantage and entitlement in the Roman Empire.

Which led to a whole new challenge.

A New Breed of Christianity

Now that the church found itself in a position of power, the challenge for the church would be to maintain its identity and sense of mission in light of this incredible development. Unfortunately, the change was so radical that the church eventually all but lost sight of its mission. Harvey puts it this way: "The eventual result of this near-fusion [of church and empire] was the loss of focus on the church's missionary identity."[9]

The expression "missionary identity" is critical. In the pre-Christendom church, every follower of Jesus understood themselves to have this "missionary identity." Their whole lives were characterized by mission—by loving their neighbors, laying their lives down for others, and living out the teachings of Jesus in their families, their friendships, their businesses, and their local communities. But with the emergence of the church's new status within the Roman Empire, a whole new understanding of "Christian" began to emerge—an understanding that stemmed in part from the fact that Constantine was neither catechized (trained in Christian theology and practice) nor baptized until shortly before his death.

Did you get that? Constantine, the first Christian Roman Emperor, was neither catechized nor baptized! Do you realize what that means?

Throughout his life as a "Christian," Constantine refused 1) to receive the teaching of the church (catechesis) and 2) to embrace Jesus' command to be baptized. As a result, "Constantine offered the world a new possibility of an unbaptized, uncatechized person who nevertheless somehow was a Christian."[10] This led to a whole new breed of Christianity, one that *did not require conversion or commitment.*

This new and unfamiliar brand of Christianity developed over a fairly short period of time. Harvey writes that before Constantine's reign, "Christians constituted a distinct minority in the empire.... Recent estimates place the percentage of Christians in the empire around 300 C.E. at about 10 percent."[11] However, this quickly changed once Constantine became a Christian. Harvey goes on to say that "within a relatively short span of time being a Christian was the accepted norm of imperial society.... By the middle of the fourth century C.E. over 50 percent of the population had been baptized."[12]

My goal here is not to portray Constantine as the bad guy of the story. No doubt, there were numerous political and cultural factors that kept Constantine from engaging in the church's catechesis and from being baptized. And I don't want to suggest that God was not involved or was not at work in the midst of all this great change. What I do want us to consider is the effect Constantine's conversion had on the church.

The church's new reality was an incredible departure from the church's pre-Constantinian existence! Suddenly, the church had political and cultural power, influence, and authority—something it had never had before. It's no wonder the church was unable to maintain its identity as a missionary people in light of such enormous change. All this newly acquired political influence must have felt like an answer to prayer. All of a sudden, there was no apparent need for mission. I can only imagine how it must have felt as the church watched thousands of people get baptized and begin to pray their prayers, not to Jupiter, but to Jesus. It must have felt like the consummation of God's plan of shalom for the world!

In little more than a moment in time, the church had been thrust into a position of cultural and political power. For the next 1500 years, that power and authority was the church's reality in the West.

And with that increase in power came a decrease in the church's missionary identity.

None of this is to say that God abandoned the church during the Christendom era or that there was zero participation in God's mission. God continued to work through his people to bring shalom into the world.

What changed was that in the pre-Christendom era, the church's missionary identity applied to *every* follower of Jesus; in Christendom, the church no longer understood its missionary identity as applying to all Christians. Only certain individuals took on the responsibility of being missional people. Only certain individuals felt called to live all of their lives all for Jesus. These people, who longed to be a part of God's mission of shalom, usually ended up living in monasteries and convents—the only model of deep discipleship available at that time. It was these monks and nuns—people like Francis of Assisi, Ignatius of Loyola, Benedict of Nursia, Hildegard of Bingen, and Teresa of Avila—who kept the light of Christ alive for the church in ways the majority of Christendom failed to. And it tended to be these monks and nuns who sought to bring shalom into the world around them, both locally and globally.

Still, most of the people who belonged to the Christendom church had no deep sense of their call to participate in God's mission. The truth is, when a person is born into a Christendom culture it's just assumed that person is a Christian. Such a person goes to church, sings the songs, prays the prayers, and pays their tithes and offerings. In Christendom, *that* is what being a Christian means. In Christendom, the kingdom of God has apparently already been established on earth. In Christendom, when you look around, you don't see any part of society that hasn't already fallen under the influence of the church. If that's the case, then if everyone in a Christendom culture is a Christian—and if God's kingdom is already established (politically and culturally, anyway)—what mission could there possibly be?

A New Distinction

Christendom affected the way the church perceived the world and its ministry to it. "In Christendom everyone is a Christian." In other words, there is no category for people who are not Christians—at least not within the Christendom society. In Christendom, babies are baptized as soon as they are born and a person belongs to a parish simply because they live in a particular village. Accordingly, there is no difference between people who have chosen of their own volition to put their faith in Christ and those who have not.

But human beings are prone to making distinctions. In Pre-Christendom, the distinction was between the church and the rest of the world—those who had yet to receive the good news of Jesus. In Christendom, there wasn't anyone who had not heard the gospel (the very basics of the gospel, in any case). As a result, in Christendom, a new distinction emerged. As Harvey puts it, in "Christendom the fundamental division is not between church and world, but between clergy and laity."[13]

This division resulted in a new caste system of sorts. Now there was a caste of Christians who were full-time spiritual leaders. There was also a caste of Christians who were spiritual followers. In other words, there were "professional" Christians and there were "ordinary" Christians.[14]

And what did these new "professional" Christians do? They provided spiritual goods and services for those who were considered to be "ordinary" Christians.

A New Reason to Exist

Because of this new distinction, ministry became something that was performed by only a select few—the clergy.

With this framework, the church's ministry no longer revolved around participating in God's mission in the world, as it had in the time before Constantine. Rather, "in Christendom societies, mission often received little emphasis, for the churches concentrate upon the pastoral care of their people and the maintenance of their structures."[15]

Sounds familiar, doesn't it?

When everyone is considered a Christian, mission seems to become obsolete. The only kind of mission that exists in Christendom culture is mission to other parts of the world. Mission is what happens far, far away. That understanding of mission continues to linger. Even today, when we think of mission, we in the Western church often imagine faraway places like Africa, Asia, and South America. We still use the language of "mission trips" to refer to *going somewhere else* to do something that God wants us to do.

In Christendom, mission at home is unnecessary. And when mission at home is no longer needed, the church must find a new reason to exist.

Historically speaking, in Christendom the purpose of the church—especially the local church—had nothing to do with reaching people with the message of Jesus and inviting them into relationship with their Creator (because "everyone is a Christian"). It had nothing to do with restoring the shalom of God to a broken and sin-scarred world. Rather, the purpose of the Christendom church was to provide spiritual goods and services to those who were considered to be ordinary—as opposed to professional—Christians.

To put it somewhat bluntly, when inviting people into the family of God became unnecessary, the Christendom church had to find other reasons to perpetuate its existence.

Christendom is Dead

So there you go. A brief summary of the effect of Christendom on the church and the mission of Jesus.

For a long time, Christendom has been a powerful force in Western society. But if you take a look around today, it sure doesn't look like Christendom anymore. Christianity no longer has a place of prominence in the nations and societies that make up Western culture. Gerhard Lohfink states that "the illusion of living in a completely Christian society has been definitively and thoroughly demolished in our day."[16]

As evidence of this, Kreider points out that "throughout most of the West, Christendom is in a state of decrepitude if not decomposition. In many countries shoppers flood the malls on Sundays, while Sunday morning has become a special time for sporting events."[17]

The death of Christendom has certainly been evident in the churches I've been a part of, and I bet it has in your church, too. Whereas the oldest generation tends to faithfully attend church every Sunday, younger generations attend far less frequently. Soccer tournaments, gymnastics competitions, weekend getaways, and professional football games on TV exert a powerful draw on younger folks in our churches. But it's not even just about declining attendance on Sunday mornings. With the death of Christendom, there has come a great loss of privilege for the church. There was a time when pastors were considered a relevant voice in discussions about public policy. There was a time when students in public schools prayed to the Christian God. There was a time when Christian witness and evangelism was held in high esteem.

Please understand, I am not condemning those who aren't in church every Sunday. I am not suggesting that we need to reclaim our political power or force children of other faiths to pray to the God of the Old and New Testaments. I am not saying we should go back to how it was. I'm pretty sure we couldn't if we tried, and if we could we probably shouldn't. What I'm saying is that these new trends—lower church attendance and less political and cultural influence—is simply evidence of our Post-Christendom reality.[18]

This new reality poses a serious challenge for churches because many churches still see the world through the framework of Christendom. Many churches still think that the old ways of reaching people—by merely focusing on providing spiritual goods and services—will be enough to keep their churches alive. If they just offer more programs, more lively worship services, better pastoral care, more exciting ministries for children and youth—then people will start coming to church again.

But, let's be honest. More and better is just not enough. More and better is probably not even what God is interested in! This is not the world it once was. Christendom—for better or for worse—is dead.

3

LUTHER'S MILKMAID

(OR LIVING YOUR SACRED CALLING)

Yes, Christendom is dead.

But that doesn't mean that some of the effects of Christendom don't continue to linger. Even though the world doesn't respond to Christianity the way it once did, Christians still tend to view the world through a Christendom-shaped lens. And that lens can get in the way of our participation in God's mission.

Which leads to this confession that I need to make. Ready?

I'm a *Star Wars* fan.

I know, I know... Who isn't a *Star Wars* fan these days? But when I say I'm a *Star Wars* fan, I mean that even during what I like to call "the desert years" of the late eighties and early nineties—when no one was even *thinking* about Star Wars—I was yearning for the day when George Lucas would finally release Episodes 1, 2, and 3. And when Episode 1 finally came out, I camped out in line for four weeks outside the Chinese Theater in Hollywood to be among the very first to see it! Was I crazy? Probably—but it was tons of fun and I met some great people! In fact, I'm still in touch today with some of the friends I made back then.

Why am I talking about *Star Wars*? Because I learned something rather profound from *Star Wars*—a concept called "dualism." Permeating the *Star Wars* universe is something called the Force. The Force has two sides, a Light Side and a Dark Side. Those connected to the Force are connected to one side or the other. A person connected to the Light Side of the Force is called a Jedi; someone connected to the Dark Side is a Sith. A person is either one or the other, but not both. *Star Wars* is full of dualisms: light and dark, good and evil, Luke and Vader, Yoda and the Emperor—even twin brother and twin sister!

The Dualism Problem

Dualism is a fancy word that basically means, "There are two things and the two things are different." If you look up dualism in the dictionary, you'll find a definition that looks something like this: *The state of being dual or consisting of two parts; division into two*. You might hear people talk about the dualism between mind and body; or spirit and matter; or good and evil.

Thinking in terms of dualisms can be helpful when it comes to separating certain things into categories (e.g., chocolate ice cream and vanilla ice cream; or east coast and west coast). These kinds of dualisms are little more than observations. I call this an "observed dualism." For instance, if I were to tell you that my shirt consists of two colors, you might observe a dualism in my shirt. Or we might observe that a twenty-four hour cycle consists of two time periods: day and night. Simple. And helpful.

But not all dualisms are created equal. There is another

kind of dualism that can be unhelpful and unhealthy. I call this a "forced dualism." It happens when we take something that shouldn't be divided, and we forcibly split it into two. And, let's be honest, we do this all the time. Human beings are prone to engage in dualistic thinking. We tend to reduce ideas and objects and people into oversimplified categories that are just not very helpful. We take a community and divide it into *this* side of the tracks and *that* side of the tracks. We take a people group and divide them into those that are "civilized" and those that are "uncivilized." We take a country and divide it into Democrats and Republicans.

Unfortunately, the church is also prone to dualistic thinking. How often have we seen churches make "us" and "them" distinctions between themselves and other churches? So often, the consequence of dualistic thinking is division in the church—Catholic/Protestant, contemporary/traditional, evangelical/progressive. I'm sure you could come up with some of your own examples.

An Unexpected Dualism

There is one particular dualism that has been a part of the church for over 1500 years. It emerged at the beginning of the Christendom era and has sadly hampered the mission of the church for all these years. It revolves around something that doesn't, at first glance, even seem to be a spiritual or theological subject. What does this dualism involve?

Work.

Yes, work. The thing that fills most of our waking hours. And not just the kind of work for which we get paid, but all kinds of work, including cleaning the house, washing the car, caring for our children, and doing our grocery shopping.

Because of humanity's tendency to engage in forced dualisms, the church has taken the unified concept of work and forcibly divided it into two categories—secular and sacred. Some work, we say, is secular work. And some work is sacred work.

Sacred work, we say, is work that is important to God. Secular work is fine, but we assume God doesn't give secular work much thought.

Luther's Milkmaid

One of the greatest losses over the course of Christian history is the understanding that every person's work is sacred. To be sure, there have been points of light throughout the Christendom era in which the sacredness of so-called "ordinary" vocations have been emphasized. During the Reformation, for instance, Martin Luther's understanding of vocation and calling elevated the work of the ordinary milkmaid and farmer to the same level as that of a monk or priest. "God is milking the cows through the vocation of the milkmaid,"[1] Luther said.

Even so, the division between those who provide "spiritual" work and those who do "ordinary" work persisted. In the centuries since the Reformation, the church has continued to subdivide the work of professional Christians from that of everyone else. And even though the emergence of the Post-Christendom era has provided the opportunity to undo that division, many today still hold on to the dualism of secular work vs. sacred work.

Christendom's Dualism

As I mentioned in the previous chapter, in Christendom everyone is assumed to be a Christian. As a result, the church emphasized the distinction, not between church and world, but between "ordinary" Christians and "special" or "professional" Christians. "Ordinary" Christians were those who did "secular" work; people like farmers, blacksmiths, merchants, and bakers. "Special" Christians were those who were engaged in "full-time" or "professional" ministry—pastors, priests, monks, nuns, missionaries, and so forth.

Two kinds of Christians: special and ordinary. Special Christians did sacred work. Ordinary Christians did secular work.

Sacred/Secular Dualism Today

In many churches today, the dualism between sacred and secular continues. Congregants often think of their role like this: show up to church, volunteer every now and then, and perhaps give financially to support the church's ministry. In their minds, however, the ministry of the church is not really their responsibility. After all, they work in the secular world. The church's ministry is the job of the church staff. It is the pastors who proclaim the gospel, conduct pastoral care, do evangelism, and provide for Christian education.

And what about missions? That certainly is not the "ordinary" Christian's job; that's the missionary's job. Or the mission pastor's job. At most, the only responsibility of the "ordinary" Christian when it comes to missions is to go on an annual short-term mission trip or to donate financially to support those who do.

Dualism Destroys the Church's Mission

Can you see why this dualism creates a problem for the church? It keeps the church from being the missional people we were meant to be. We end up with 1) "special" or "professional" Christians who are paid to carry out the mission of the church and live their lives in the realm of the "sacred," and 2) "ordinary" Christians who show up for church once a week, but live most of their lives in the realm of the "secular."

In the end, the mission of Jesus loses out. Why? Because only a few of his people are actually working to fulfill his mission.

If we are to carry out God's mission—the mission to bring healing and wholeness to the entire world—if the church is going to incarnate God's love to the world so that the world will flourish as God intends, then we must work to dismantle the dualism of the sacred and the secular. We must help people understand that *all* of life is meant to be lived *all* for Jesus.

It's a Discipleship Issue

The problem of dualism becomes an issue of discipleship and spiritual formation. If we think God does not value our work or if we don't think of God as being present with us in the doing of our work, we are far less likely to feel connected to God or listen for God's leading when we are not doing so-called sacred church stuff. It maintains the illusion that God is interested only in the spiritual church stuff we do once or twice a week. And it keeps us from developing a deeper relationship with our Creator because we live with the assumption that God isn't really interested in the majority of our lives.

One of the great challenges for the church today, therefore, is to undo the dualism of the sacred and the secular—for the sake of the church and for the sake of the world.

Miscommunication

As a pastor, I have to be really intentional about reminding my people that their vocations are sacred. It's so easy to forget about that. Not because I don't value the work my people do during the week or because I don't think my people can't do good for the kingdom of God while they are at work. I do.

However—whether intentionally or unintentionally—there is a tendency to communicate the following message to my people:

> *Get a good job. Go to work. Earn a good salary if you can. Work hard and with integrity because you're a Christian. If there's a Bible study at work, get involved in the Bible study—that's a good, sacred thing you can do at work. Share your faith—that's a good, sacred thing you can do at work. And invite people to church. Oh, yes—invite people to church! That's definitely a good, sacred thing you can do at work.*
>
> *But when you're not at work, make sure you come to church because this is where the sacred stuff really happens. And be sure to bring some of your money to church because this is where the sacred stuff really happens.*

Unfortunately, that leaves people with the impression that

what they do Monday through Saturday is far less valuable in God's eyes than what happens on Sunday morning. When we communicate this message from the pulpit—whether directly or indirectly, intentionally or unintentionally—people become less inclined to draw near to God and are less aware of how God is at work through their vocation.

How We Feed the Sacred/Secular Divide

I remember hearing a pastor say to his congregation at the beginning of a worship service, "This next hour is the most important hour of your week."

I'll tell you what—as a pastor of a congregation I really want to believe that! And there's a part of me that really wants my people to believe it, too. I want them to know how crucial that one hour of worship on Sunday morning is. This isn't just an hour of "going to church"—*this is the most important hour of the week.*

But is it really? No doubt, the weekly worship service is important. I'd even go so far as to say that it is *one of* the most important parts of the week for followers of Jesus.

But is the worship service the most important hour of the week? Well, that's debatable.

Consider the logic behind this claim:

1. Worshiping God at church on Sunday mornings is a sacred thing.
2. All the other things you do the rest of the week are secular things.
3. Doing sacred things is better than doing secular things.
4. The sacred thing we do on Sunday morning advances the mission of God.

5. The secular stuff you do the rest of the week doesn't really matter to God.
6. God is more pleased by the sacred thing you do on Sunday morning than all the other things you do the rest of the week.

While we might not state this conclusion in these words, it is this logic that perpetuates the forced dualism of the sacred and the secular that we find in so many churches.

Re-Integrating the Sacred and the Secular

One of the greatest challenges for the church today is the re-integration of the sacred and the secular. Too many people live with the false belief that their Monday through Saturday lives are less important to God than their life on Sunday, especially Sunday morning. Too many people think that only pastors and missionaries and evangelists and worship leaders have a calling from God.

This is simply not true. Every person has a calling from God. In fact, every person has a *sacred* calling. Why? Because every human being has been called by God to steward the world and to bring healing and wholeness into the world.

A helpful way to think about your calling is to think of it as two distinct, yet totally integrated callings—your *primary calling* and your *secondary calling*.

Primary Calling

Our primary calling is exactly the same for every person. *Your* primary calling is exactly the same as *my* primary calling. It is also the exact same as the Pope's primary calling, as the President's primary calling, and as Oprah Winfrey's primary calling. Our primary calling is *to be in relationship with the One who calls us.* This is the calling of every human being that has ever lived.[2]

We see this primary calling right from creation. As soon as human beings are created, they enter into relationship with the God who made them. The very act of creation itself has relational overtones; God "breathed into his nostrils the breath of life, and the man became a living being" (Genesis 2:6). There is deep connection—an exchange of breath—between Creator and creation right from the beginning.

When sin enters the story, it becomes clear that both God and humanity are in agony over their broken relationship. Adam and Eve hide in shame as God cries out, "Where are you?!"

It is into this relationship between Creator and creation —between Caller and called—that we are invited. Moreover, God invites us into relationship with his Son, the Savior. Paul says in 1 Corinthians 1:9, "God is faithful, who has called you into fellowship with his Son, Jesus Christ our Lord." And Jesus himself calls us to himself: "Come to me, all you who are weary and burdened, and I will give you rest" (Matthew 11:28). Our primary calling is to be in relationship with the God who created us, loves us, and saves us.

Secondary Calling

The call to be in relationship with God our Creator is our primary calling. Notice the verb in that last statement. The call is to *be* in relationship with God. Our primary calling has to do with *who we are*—children of God created in the image of God, created to live in relationship with our Heavenly Father.

Our secondary calling has to do with *what we do*. It is the call to participate with God in stewarding this world.

In Genesis 2, we are told that when God created the world, "there was no one to work the ground" (Genesis 2:5). There was no one to join God in realizing God's desire for creation. So God created a human being and "put him in the Garden of Eden to work it and take care of it" (Genesis 2:15).

This is our secondary calling: to participate with God in caring for the world that God has made. Another word for this is *work*. Teachers, through their work, participate with God in stewarding the world. Chefs, through their work, participate with God in stewarding the world. Electricians, through their work, participate with God in stewarding the world.

But our jobs are not our only callings. Each person has multiple callings. You may have a calling as a software engineer or a plumber or a business person. And through that calling, you participate with God in bringing shalom into the world. At the same time, you may have a calling as a mom or a dad or as a grandparent. You also likely have a calling as a neighbor in your neighborhood and as a citizen of your country. Through each of these callings, you work to steward this world and restore the shalom that was broken.

Remember that each of these callings is a *sacred* calling. Each calling is one of the ways in which God works through you to accomplish God's mission in the world. Teachers accomplish God's mission of bringing shalom into the world by instilling knowledge and confidence in their students. Plumbers work toward the restoration of shalom in our broken world by keeping it clean and sanitary—and when we see parts of the world that have sewage running through the streets, we think to ourselves, "That's not what God wants for the world!" Moms and dads and grandparents participate in the mission of God by loving well their children and grandchildren, raising them to become healthy adults, teaching them to love and care for others. As neighbors we bring shalom into our neighborhoods by serving our neighbors. And as citizens, we vote and/or engage in ways that we believe will make our nation better and our world safer for all.

Every secondary calling is *sacred* because it is through our various callings that we participate with God to bring healing and wholeness into the world. This is why Paul can say, "And whatever you do, whether in word or deed, do it *all* in the name of the Lord Jesus, giving thanks to God the Father through him" (Colossians 3:17, italics added).

More Than a Job

Our primary calling is to be in relationship with the Caller. Our secondary calling is to participate with God in stewarding, blessing, and healing this world. And while participating in God's mission is the calling of every person, the ways we live it out are utterly unique to each individual.

These unique ways in which we live out our secondary callings are what we call our *vocations*.

I used to think of vocation as nothing more than a job. When I was in high school, I had friends who went to a place called "Vo-Tech" in the afternoons, which was short for "Vocational Technology." There they learned various skills that would help them get a job after high school. And that's what a vocation was, as far as I knew—it was just a job.

But your vocation is so much more than your job.

Your vocations are the unique ways in which God has called you to bring healing and wholeness into the world. They are how God has shaped you to live out your secondary calling. In fact, the word "vocation" itself technically has nothing to do with work; it comes from the Latin word, *vocare*, which means, "to call." We also get the English word, "voice" from *vocare*—as well as "vocal" and "vociferous" (one of my all-time favorite words!).

Your vocations, then, are what you have been called to do in response to the *voice* of the One who calls you.

You Have Multiple Vocations

You may have noticed that I keep using the plural *vocations*, rather than the singular *vocation*. That's because just as we have more than one secondary calling, we have more than one vocation.

God calls us to bring healing and wholeness—or *shalom* —into the world in a variety of ways. You may have a vocation as mother or father, as grandmother or grandfather, as son or daughter, as neighbor, citizen, student, retiree, and so forth.

And, yes, one of your vocations involves the *work* that you do for a living.

Your Vocation is Sacred

If we have these various vocations, which are our response to God's call, then there is something sacred about what we do. Our vocations are the ways in which we participate in God's mission of restoring shalom to a broken and hurting world. As you can see, an understanding of vocation as a response to God's call—i.e., a theology of vocation—helps to undo the sacred/secular dualism that we talked about earlier.

It is so important to recognize the sacredness of each person's vocation. Why? Because:

- When a business-person understands their work as a divine vocation, they begin to understand that their calling is to restore shalom to the world by facilitating the transfer of both necessary and delightful goods and services.
- When a lawyer understands their work as a divine vocation, they begin to understand that their calling is to restore shalom to the world by working for justice.
- When a trash collector understands their work as a divine vocation, they begin to understand that their calling is to restore shalom to the world by making the world clean and beautiful and sanitary.

As a result, work is no longer simply a job—it is the way we do ministry in the world. The places where we work, eat, sleep, and play—our *vocational spheres*—are the places where God invites us to join him in bringing shalom into the world. Our vocational spheres are also the places where we can begin to discern how God is already at work in the world and how God might be inviting the church to join in his mission in new ways.

As we develop a healthy theology of vocation, we begin to understand that ministry doesn't happen only on Sunday mornings and it isn't performed only by a few special Christians (pastors, priests, missionaries, etc.). Rather, we become aware that ministry is happening in every nook and cranny of the world. It means that all kinds of people are participating with God in bringing healing and wholeness into the world—often without even knowing it.

It means that ministry happens wherever God's people are living out their vocations!

Doing Church Stuff

Allow me to shift the conversation just for a moment by asking a question. What kinds of things do churches generally tend to do in order to help their people grow in their faith? Here are a few things we have done in the churches I've served. We:

- Held worship services.
- Sang worship songs.
- Participated in small groups.
- Asked people to usher and serve coffee on Sunday mornings.
- Engaged in mission projects, both local and global.
- Encouraged people to read their Bible and pray during the week.

In other words, we invited them to do a lot of church stuff.

These are all good and valuable to the church's ministry, but, believe it or not, if we're not careful they can also be very limiting to a person's spiritual development. Even if a person did all of these things, they would only comprise a few hours a week. What about the rest of the week? There is a lot of "formation" going on from other cultural sources during all those other hours in the week.

So... How can people be spiritually formed, not only when they are doing church stuff, but also when they are at work or in class or around the dinner table?

All of Life is Spiritual

Emphasizing only the few hours in a week that people are doing church stuff will rarely lead to deep inner life spiritual transformation.

This is why focusing on a person's various vocations as sacred callings (both their primary and secondary callings) is so critical. It is as we live out our vocations that the Spirit of God can form us into the kind of people we were created to be.

When an electrician understands their work as a sacred calling... When a babysitter understands their work as a sacred calling... When a grandparent understands their care for their grandchildren as a sacred calling... When a lawyer or business person or coffee barista understands their work as a sacred calling...

Well, that changes everything!

All of a sudden, your spiritual life is no longer limited to the stuff you do when you're at church or in your small group. No longer are you growing in your faith only when you're engaged in explicitly spiritual activities. No longer are you serving God only when you're participating in what's on the church calendar. Now, all of life becomes the realm of the spiritual. Now, God is understood to be present all the time—not just when we're at church. Now, even your job and your family and your school and your neighborhood are the locus of spiritual transformation and discipleship.

What Can Churches Do?

At this point, you may be thinking, "Yeah, that sounds great! But how do I help people see the sacredness of their vocations? What can my church do to help people live into their callings—their sacred callings—as parent, neighbor, student, and employer or employee? And is there some way that the church can support them, learn from them, and perhaps find new ways of blessing the world in and through the vocational spheres of our people?"

These questions are so important. And we're going to address these questions quite specifically in Chapter 5 with something I call a Vocational Connection Group. I'll explain what that is and how to implement one—start to finish—in your church or ministry.

But right now what I'd like to do is touch on one more important concept before we get into the nuts and bolts of a Vocational Connection Group. Without this, a Vocational Connection Group would be utterly futile. I'm talking about the sovereignty of God.

4

FINDING CHRIST IN THE SITUATION

(OR GOD IS AHEAD OF US)

Did you know that in ancient England, women believed they could stay young by carrying around an acorn? And in Spain, people will eat twelve grapes on New Year's Eve for good luck (at least, that's what Google tells me!). In Japan, people tuck their thumbs in when passing a graveyard in order to protect their parents from death (the Japanese word for thumb literally means "parent finger"). And in some cultures (you'll never believe this!), in order to keep bad luck away (I'm telling you, this is crazy!) people will *knock on wood!*

Why do we do this? Why do people act on these funny little superstitions? I suspect it's because these superstitions give us a small sense that we are in control of our lives. So, we throw salt over our shoulders and keep our umbrellas closed indoors.

But logic tells us that superstitions don't actually give us any control. And many of us don't really believe in superstitions, anyway. Even so, there are things that we do—more logical and respectable things, some would say—that give us the feeling that we have control over our lives. For instance, we:

- Get a good education.
- Get a good job.
- Earn lots of money.
- Buy insurance.
- Exercise and eat healthy.
- Put our kids in good schools.

There is, of course, nothing wrong with going to a good school or getting a well-paying job or doing cardio. These are good things. The fact is, however, they don't give us nearly as much control as we would like to think.

But there is One who does have control. There is One who holds both the world and our lives in his hands. There is One who is—to use a theological word—sovereign.

The Sovereignty of God

When I talk about the sovereignty of God, I'm referring to the reality that God can and will do as God chooses. The concept of God's sovereignty is something we see throughout the scriptures. The Psalmist, for instance, writes, "The Lord does whatever pleases him, in the heavens and on the earth, in the seas and all their depths" (Psalm 135:6). Isaiah says, "I make known the end from the beginning, from ancient times, what is still to come. I say, 'My purpose will stand, and I will do all that I please'" (Isaiah 46:10). And in Philippians 2:13, in the New Testament, Paul teaches the sovereignty of God when he writes to the church in Philippi that "it is God who works in you to will and to act in order to fulfill his good purpose."

I realize the notion of God's sovereignty raises a lot of questions. If God is good, why does God allow evil in the world? If God is all-powerful, why doesn't God always prevent catastrophes from happening? And what about free will? If God is sovereign, how much freedom to choose do we actually have? Those are big questions and this is not a long book, so I'm not going to try to address those questions here. And while the issue of God's sovereignty can leave us scratching our heads, the next sentence is one I can write with great certainty.

In the end, God's will is going to be accomplished.

Whew... What a relief! Knowing that God is in control takes a huge load off of me. It reminds me, not only that my life is in God's care, but also that the healing of the world doesn't ultimately depend on me. The mission of God doesn't rely on my influence or expertise or creativity or perseverance. The world is in God's hands and God will ultimately bring full and complete healing, wholeness, and restoration to the world.

Joseph's Story

The sovereignty of God reminds me, not only that God is in control, but also that God is already ahead of us working out his will in the world. We see this reality throughout the scriptures. God's sovereign activity is evident, for instance, throughout the story of Joseph in Genesis 37 through 50.

Since you're the kind of person who is interested in reading this book, I suspect you already know the story. But I'll summarize it for you anyway. Joseph, the eleventh and favorite son of Jacob, is sold into slavery by his envious brothers. While a slave in Egypt, Joseph rises to power by means of his integrity and God-inspired wisdom.

Eventually, he becomes second in command only to Pharaoh.

In the end, Joseph saves not only the lives of Egypt and the surrounding nations but also the lives of his brothers and father. Joseph affirms God's sovereign action throughout his life—including through the sinful actions of his brothers—when he says, "You intended to harm me, but God intended it for good to accomplish what is now being done, the saving of many lives" (Genesis 50:20).

God's "Previousness" in the Old Testament

To affirm the doctrine of God's sovereignty is to affirm that God is in control and that God is already at work in the world ahead of us.

Isn't that amazing? Isn't it incredible to think that God is already doing a work in places and in lives that are yet untouched by the church?

The famed missiologist, Lesslie Newbigin, refers to this as "the previousness of the kingdom."[1] This previousness is evident throughout the scriptures. The stories of Joseph and Daniel, for instance, tell of a God who gives dreams to pagan kings (Genesis 41:1-7; Daniel 2:1, 4:10-17). It isn't until after God has been at work in the lives of these kings that Joseph and Daniel (that is, the people of God) are invited to join in God's work by interpreting the dreams (Genesis 41:25-32; Daniel 2:29-45; 4:20-27).

But it is not only in the lives of kings that God is ahead of his people. God is and has been at work beyond the people of God in all kinds of ways. God worked, for instance, through a pagan prostitute, Rahab, when God handed the city of Jericho over to the Israelites (Joshua 2:1-24; 5:24-25). Ruth, a Moabite woman, was another outsider in whose life

God was active—in this case, to bless her Israelite mother-in-law, Naomi (Ruth 4:14-15), as well as to become the great grandmother of King David (Ruth 4:21-22).

But wait, there's more! God worked through these two women—Rahab and Ruth—in an even more astounding way. The gospel writer, Matthew, tells us that these two women were ancestors of Jesus, God's Messiah (Matthew 1:5).

When we read the Old Testament, we see that God is clearly capable of accomplishing his will in the world well before his people decide it's time to get involved. God is always at work in the world ahead of his people.

God's "Previousness" in the New Testament

It isn't only in the Old Testament that we see God ahead of his people. God goes before his people throughout the New Testament, as well. Let me give you a couple of examples.

When Peter receives an invitation to the house of the Roman centurion, Cornelius—a Gentile!—Peter finds that the Holy Spirit has already been at work in Cornelius' household (Acts 10:22). As Peter begins to speak to Cornelius' family, he finds that he is doing little more than participating with what God is already doing. He watches with amazement while "the gift of the Holy Spirit" is poured out on all those listening to him (Acts 10:45).

A little later, the apostles find that the Gentile city of Antioch is already full of Christians, thanks to "men from Cyprus and Cyrene, [who] went to Antioch and began to speak to Greeks also, telling them the good news about the Lord Jesus" (Acts 11:20). Apparently, God was already calling people to follow Christ before the apostles ever have a clue!

The existence of the church in Antioch eventually leads

to a significant meeting of the apostles and elders in Jerusalem. After much wrestling over whether or not Gentiles should be required to be circumcised according to Jewish law, the apostles and church leaders ultimately decide, under the leadership of James, that since God has *already* given the Holy Spirit to the Gentiles, then there seems to be no reason to require circumcision (Acts 15:1-20).

This event was a key moment in the life of the church. Because the apostles were open to seeing what God was already doing out in the world, they were able to make a critical shift. Rather than holding on to the gospel as something that was only for Jews or Jewish converts, the apostles were able to welcome Gentiles directly into the family of God without any prerequisites (e.g., circumcision). The apostles were in tune with what God was initiating and, thus, were able to adapt to what God was already doing.

We Are Invited to Join God

If we see examples of God at work ahead of his people throughout the scriptures, what does that mean for us today? Could it mean that God is at work ahead of his people still today?

Yes!

We can be sure that there is no place where God is not already present in some way. God's activity in the world is limited neither to the geographical location nor the personal interests of God's people. Yes, God calls the church to participate with him in his mission. But God is not dependent on the church to accomplish his mission. As a result, we don't need to be anxious about the success of the church's ministry. We don't need to feel like we have failed

God or failed the world if somehow the work we do doesn't seem as effective as we would like it to be.

The church's ministry never truly initiates anything—it only gets involved in God's already-in-progress ministry. That's why I love this quote from Lesslie Newbigin: "The church's witness is secondary and derivative. The church is witness insofar as it follows obediently where the Spirit leads".[2]

"Secondary and derivative." Strange words. They almost sound derogatory, don't they? As though there were something more important than the church's witness.

There is only one thing that could be more important than the church's witness—the activity of the Spirit of God in the world. The church's ministry is "secondary and derivative" because its ministry *derives* from the Spirit's leading.

Ministry success can be measured, then, not in terms of size or numbers, but in terms of the church's obedience to the Spirit. Robert Schreiter, in *Constructing Local Theologies,* puts it like this: "The prevailing mode of evangelization and church development should be one of *finding Christ in the situation* rather than concentrating on bringing Christ into the situation"[3] (italics added). But this only becomes possible when God's people take steps to become aware of what God is doing in the world.

So often, churches try to figure out how to bring Christ to their communities. But what if our calling is not to bring Christ into our communities—as though he were not already there? What if our calling is simply to *join God* in what God is *already doing*?

Pastors Can't Know It All

But this involves a significant paradigm shift, both for church members and especially for church leaders. Yes, God is already at work out in the neighborhood and the world. But how can church leaders discover what God is up to out there beyond the walls of the church?

As a pastor, I spend a lot of my time with church folks. That's not a bad thing. That's my calling. I work with our staff, with our elders, with our deacons. I meet with other pastors in our presbytery for regional leadership. I visit church members in the hospital and pray with them in my office.

While I do have some relationships with people outside our church, the reality is that most of my interactions with people revolve around my work in the church. If you're a pastor, I suspect that may be the case for you, too. And even if you do have a lot of contact with non-church folks (and good for you if you do!), you are still only one person. The question is, how can one person discover all the many ways God is at work in one's community? To what extent can one who spends most of their time with church folks become aware of God's activity in people's lives outside the church?

The reality is that many pastors and church staff—because they are focused on the ministry to which God called them within the church—simply don't have the capacity to discover all that God is doing outside the church. Again, this is not a bad thing. The beauty of the church is that we are one Body with many parts. Some of us are called to serve within the church and others are called to serve outside the church. This is great news because it means that God has his people *out there*—all over the place!

The Advantage of the Body of Christ

While pastors tend to engage mostly with people in their congregation, church members tend to engage mostly with people outside the congregation. This is a tremendous advantage that I believe God intends to leverage for his mission in the world. Think about it. God's people go to the gym with people who are not a part of the church. They take their kids to birthday parties where the moms and dads are not a part of the church. They are involved in community organizations in which most of the people are not a part of the church.

And here's the big one:

They work at their jobs with people who are not a part of the church.

That's forty or more hours per week during which members of Christ's Body are actively engaged outside the church!

Why is this so important? Because it is those congregants with their "ordinary" and "secular" jobs who have a first-hand view of what God is doing "out there." As they engage in their vocational spheres, participating with God in bringing shalom into the world through the various kinds of work that they do, they have the opportunity to discern God's activity in and through the places of their vocations. When God's people listen, observe, and converse with co-workers, clients, supervisors, and employees, they get a unique glimpse into what God is up to in the lives of people who are outside the church.

Becoming Intentionally Aware of God's Activity

The question is, how do we help God's people be intentionally alert to what God is doing out there? Most of us tend to move through our days without really thinking about how God is active around us. How can we better tune in to the Spirit of God at work in the lives of the people we interact with every day?

Paying attention to what God is up to requires intentionality. It is so easy for followers of Jesus to miss God's activity in their work places and other places of vocation if they are focused only on meeting their obligations, hitting their numbers, making sure their customers are happy, and so forth. To have eyes to see, God's people need to always be asking, "Where is God at work in this person or this situation?"

Please don't misunderstand me. In no way am I suggesting that there is no inherent value in the work our people do in and of itself. There absolutely is! Our work is our vocation, our sacred calling. It is the way God has called us to participate in what God is doing in the world. That calling includes both the work we have been hired to do *and* the work of paying attention to what God is doing in, around, and beyond the actual work.

So...

Is there a way for the church to help congregants become intentional about noticing what God is up to in their workplace and in the lives of those with whom they interact day in and day out?

Can we help a barista notice what God is doing in the life of that mom who comes in for coffee every day? Can we help a salesperson discern the deeper needs of her clients?

Can we help the little league coach pay attention to what God is up to in the lives of his players and their families?

The answer is yes! There *is* a way. And it comes in the form of something I like to call Vocational Connection Groups.

Introducing Vocational Connection Groups

If the previousness of God is really a thing—if God really is at work in the world ahead of his people—then there must be a way to discern what God is up to. There must be a way to discover how God is inviting us to participate in the mission of God. There must be a way to harness the power of the vocations and callings of all of God's people to help the church find out what God is doing "out there." There must be a way for churches to escape the captivity of just doing the same old ministry programs again and again because, well, that's the way we've always done things.

A Vocational Connection Group (VCG) can help church members become intentionally aware of what God is doing "out there." VCGs are a way for churches to foster a growing awareness among congregants of how God is at work in people's lives outside the church. It can also help pastors and other church leaders get a sense of what God is up to in the community and the city in which their congregation is located. VCGs can even spark the imaginations of churches as they discover new and fresh ways of joining God in his mission.

What exactly is a Vocational Connection Group and how does it work? That's exactly what we will look at in Part 2 of this book.

PART II

ENGAGING YOUR CHURCH IN GOD'S MISSION

5

BEYOND THINGIFICATION

(OR A METHOD FOR JOINING GOD'S MISSION)

I grew up in the church. When I was a kid, it seemed like everybody went to church. Sunday services were always full and there was plenty of church stuff to do throughout the week.

But since I've become a pastor, that just hasn't been the reality of the churches I've served. Sunday mornings are often far from full and getting people to participate in weekday activities feels like pulling teeth. The culture has changed. We no longer live in a Christendom world. We no longer live in a world in which maintaining the institution of the church is easy. We live in a Post-Christendom world in which the church is simply not on most people's radar.

Unfortunately, we don't yet know how to be the church in a Post-Christendom culture. Yes, some churches seem to know exactly how to do church in today's context. Some churches are growing and seem to have lots of success. But they are in the vast minority of churches today. And who knows how long that apparent success will last?

For most of our churches, we live in a time in which we need to do a lot of learning, a lot of growing spiritually, and a lot of experimenting. We need to learn from our neighbors, from each other, and from God. And how do we do that? How do we learn? By listening. By paying attention to what God is doing in our neighbors' lives, by paying attention to what God is saying to us through our brothers and sisters in the faith, and by paying attention to God as he speaks to our hearts and makes himself personally known to us.

We need to allow our lives to be formed by God as we listen. If we're going to be the church God wants us to be, we each have to be open to being shaped into the person God created us to be. We call this spiritual formation, and it happens as we daily surrender ourselves to Jesus.

We also need to *try stuff out*. Again, we can't simply assume people will get involved in our churches. The old programs and strategies—like catchy sermon series, special guest speakers, BBQ dinners, and movie nights—are less likely to resonate with or attract people today than they were fifty, thirty, or even ten years ago. What kinds of ministries, outreaches, or programs will connect with people today? Who knows?!

And maybe "resonating with," "attracting," and "connecting with" isn't really the goal. Maybe the goal isn't to figure out what connects with people so they start coming to our churches. Maybe the goal is to discover what God is doing in the world and how we are being invited to participate in the mission of God.

Vocational Connection Groups

What is God doing in the world?

How are we invited to join God in what God is already doing?

These are the questions that a Vocational Connection Group (VCG) is intended to answer. A Vocational Connection Group is meant to help people listen—really listen—to their neighbors, to each other, and to God. In so doing, a deeper faith is developed in the participants. God becomes more real and more present to each individual. And as the group deepens its relationship with God, VCG participants are better able to discern how God is at work in the lives of their neighbors, leading to ministry experiments through which they will discern even more deeply how God is calling them and their church to join in God's mission in the world.

What Does "Vocational Connection Group" Mean?

Implementing a Vocational Connection Group (or, better yet, several VCGs over time) could be the key that unlocks your church's ability to discern how God is calling your church to engage its community.

But what does "Vocational Connection Group" mean? Sounds like a pretty cumbersome name for a church group. I use this name because it is descriptive of what the VCG does. (If you do one in your church, you can give it whatever name you want!)

I call it a Vocational Connection Group because it involves three activities:

1. *Living into our* **vocations**. As God's people, we are called to live out our various callings—as moms and dads, as employees and employers, as business people and soccer coaches. We live out our callings every single day. A Vocational Connection Group taps into what people are

already doing, rather than asking them to take on something new or add something to their already full schedule.

2. **Connecting** *with people.* As we live into our vocations, we are bound to interact with people —people who are loved by God and in whose lives God is already at work.
3. *Meeting with other church members in a* **group** to reflect on what God is up to in and around our vocations and to discover together how we are being invited to participate in God's mission in the world.

Origin Story

The idea for Vocational Connection Groups emerged from my Doctor of Ministry work several years ago. Completion of a Doctor of Ministry involves doing a project in one's congregation and then writing a dissertation based on that project. My project involved something that, at the time, I called Neighborhood Connection Groups.

My goal in that project was to get 10-20 people from my congregation involved in neighborhood groups or activities with the purpose of getting to know our neighbors and discerning how God might be inviting our church to join in God's mission in our community. I called them Neighborhood Connection Groups because the focus was intended to be on our neighborhood. We were a neighborhood church and we wanted to engage our neighborhood more deeply.

Why do I now refer to them as Vocational Connection Groups? Because I've come to believe that engaging our neighbors can happen beyond our neighborhoods. In fact, connecting with neighbors can happen anywhere that we are engaged in our vocations.

Every church is filled with people who have been called by God to be in relationship with him and to participate in God's mission to bring healing and wholeness to the world. It is through their callings, their vocations, that God works to restore shalom in our broken world. So, for churches who don't happen to have a neighborhood-focused DNA, thinking about their mission in terms of their vocational spheres may be more helpful. That's one of the reasons I changed the name from Neighborhood Connection Group to Vocational Connection Group. (I realize there is an argument to be made that all churches should be neighborhood-focused. I believe it is important, however, to begin with where churches *are* in terms of their neighborhood engagement, rather than where they should be.)

The other reason I changed the name has to do with the fact that when we are talking about a neighborhood activity, we're really talking about a vocation. The reason I wanted people to be involved in a neighborhood activity is because I believed that was a place where God was (and is) at work. But God is at work in other places, too. God is at work in my son's basketball team, which holds practices and has games all over San Diego. God is at work in the Toastmaster's group which may meet in the next town over. God is at work in my job, to which I may have to commute thirty minutes each way. Each of these is a vocation and a domain in which we are invited to participate in the mission of God.

So I decided that it would be more helpful to think of this group as a *Vocational* Connection Group than a *Neighborhood* Connection Group.

"Is It Possible?"

Before we dig into the specifics of how a Vocational Connection Group works, let me ask three questions to get us thinking. These questions address three big concerns almost every church wrestles with: 1) the importance of identifying people's real needs, 2) the hope of discovering how God is already at work in the world, and 3) the desire to do what God is calling us to do.

These three questions are questions of possibility. Is it even possible to accomplish the kinds of things that a Vocational Connection Group is meant to address? Here are the three questions:

1. *Is it possible to discover what people in our neighborhood and vocational spheres actually need and where God wants to meet their need?*

Churches sometimes think they know just what a community's needs are. We may think our community needs a solution to the homeless problem. Or people need financial guidance. Or there is a need for better schools. Or people need a relationship with God.

These may all be true—maybe people in our neighborhoods do need these things (and, of course, everyone does need to be in relationship with their Creator)—but there may be a whole lot more need about which we have no idea. Perhaps there's a need to deal with alcoholism, but it's hard to see that if everyone is putting on a perfect smile. Perhaps there's a need to help parents love their kids well, which can be very difficult to see without someone opening up about it. Can the church discover, not only the felt needs, but the deep down needs that are harder to see?

2. *Is it possible to discover what God is up to in our neighborhood and places of vocation?*

We know God is up to something—he always is! But what? It can be really hard to identify what God is doing in the lives of neighbors, colleagues, classmates, and even friends. How can we discover what it is that God is up to in people's lives and in our vocational spheres?

3. *Is it possible to discover how God wants to work through us in light of our own gifts, passions, and callings?*

Every church is unique because the people in each church are unique. So, how does God want to use the unique abilities, resources, and networks that we have been graced with in our local church? Can we discover the specific ways in which God wants to work through us as this particular congregation in this particular time and place?

Yes!

The answers to these three questions are: Yes, yes, and yes! Vocational Connection Groups make it possible for your church to:

1. Discover the needs of your neighborhood and vocational spheres.
2. Become aware of what God is up to in your community.
3. Discern how God wants to work through your congregation's unique gifts, resources, and callings.

But here's the rub. It's not easy to make these discoveries. It requires a lot more than taking a congregational survey or purchasing demographic data to uncover what God is up to. These may be helpful (and relatively easy to do), but they are simply not enough.

So, how do we do it? How do we go about discovering where and how God is at work? We can do it through a process of *action* and *reflection*.

Action and Reflection

The goal of a Vocational Connection Group is not only to discover how God is at work in the world, but also to shape the way followers of Jesus think about ministry in the world, to develop them into the kind of people who are growing in awareness of God's activity in their place of work, in their school, in their family, in their neighborhood, or wherever they live out their God-given vocations. Why? So that, more and more, they become the kind of people who naturally live out their calling in light of God's mission. There is a kind of "renewing of the mind" that takes place through the Vocational Connection Group process.

But a new way of thinking doesn't just happen. While the transfer of information about Jesus, God, the Bible, and ministry in the form of sermons, Bible studies, books, and so forth can be formative for a person, it takes something much deeper for new thinking to emerge. What shapes a person's thinking is a process of *action* and *reflection*—a process that involves *doing* something, and then sitting back to *consider* what happened and what might be done next, followed by more action, and, again, more reflection. It is this back and forth between action and reflection that allows people's thinking to develop in new ways.

The *action* part in the action-reflection process is the easy part. Many of us are good at the action portion because many of us are good at doing stuff. Tell me what to do and I'll do it. And when I'm done doing it, I'll be able to say, "Look! I did it!" But real transformation and discovery doesn't happen just by doing stuff.

Let me give you an example. Churches love doing mission trips. One of my former congregations used to do an annual mission trip to Mexico where we would build a house for a family in need. Definitely a worthwhile endeavor! And it always gave the mission team a real feeling of accomplishment and significance. At the end of the mission trip we could look at the house we had built with our own hands. We could touch and feel the tangible evidence of our work. And we saw the smiles on the faces of those we had served.

But then what? What do we do when we get back home? For some people, a weekend mission trip like this can be a transformative experience. But many others just go back to their regular lives without any real inner life transformation. There hasn't been any real change in their thinking about poverty, about systemic injustice, about how to address the systems that sustain poverty, or about how they themselves may be called to engage the problem of poverty.

So often, we not only fail to help people live out in their day-to-day lives the kind of good work they have done on a mission trip, but we also fail to nurture renewed thinking or surrendered hearts. But what if the mission team continued to meet monthly? What if they took time, not only to remember stories from the mission trip, but also to tell new stories of how God was working through them in their workplace, in their family, and in their neighborhood? What if they told and retold with one another the stories of

God's activities in the Scriptures? And what if they continued to pray not only for those they served on the mission trip, but for all those whom they serve in their various vocations?

Can you see the power of adding reflection to action? Reflection is what helps action become deeply rooted in our lives. In other words:

Action + Reflection = Transformation

Reflection is so important because it completes the circle. Robert Schreiter, in *Constructing Local Theologies*, says, "Good reflection leads to action, and action is not completed until it has been reflected upon."[1]

In the Vocational Connection Group process, action-reflection looks like this: We start by thinking about where to get involved in our community (at work, at our kids' school, at the YMCA, etc.) and make a decision to intentionally pay attention to people there. That's reflection. Then we take action by going to work, going to school, going to the YMCA, and interacting with people, listening to their stories, and taking note of what God might be doing in their lives. But we can't stop there; we have to reflect together on what we experienced and learned during our time of action. Only then does real change begin to take root in our lives.

Action

The action part of the Vocational Connection Group's action-reflection process includes essentially two things: going and listening.

1. *Going:* A Vocational Connection Group involves going to work, going to school, going to the gym, going to your kids' little league practice, going to the PTA meeting, and so forth. It means engaging in your vocation—your calling—in your work, with your family, in your community, and so forth.
2. *Listening:* Action also involves actively listening to the stories people are telling. What are your co-workers struggling with? What are the other soccer parents excited about? What do your neighbors find frustrating? Action involves having conversations, asking questions, and listening for what God might be up to below the surface in people's lives.

Drop the Agenda

It's usually a good idea to have a plan. If you're starting a church or a business, beginning an exercise program, or moving into a new career you should probably have a plan. You should know how much it's going to cost, how long it will take, who will help you accomplish it, and what the end result will be. It's important to set your agenda.

But there are times when you are better off not having an agenda.

A Vocational Connection Group is one of those times. One of the critical components in discerning what God is up to is letting go of our own preconceived plans, our own expectations and assumptions, in order to be open to whatever God might want to reveal. As a result, VCG participants must not go into their vocational activity with an agenda focused on things like sharing their faith, converting people to Christianity, or inviting people to church.

The purpose of a VCG is not to increase the church's attendance or membership; rather, it is to discover how God's Spirit is already at work in the hearts and minds of neighbors, colleagues, and friends. The only agenda the Vocational Connection Group participants should have is to simply participate in their vocational activity and listen to people's stories whenever they are engaged in conversation.

But is that what Jesus would want? To have us go out without an agenda?

Well, if you look at the New Testament, when Jesus sends out his disciples to engage with people in neighboring villages, he sends them without an agenda. He tells them to visit nearby towns without "a purse or bag or sandals" (Luke 10:4). He instructs them to stay wherever they are welcomed (Luke 10:7) and to receive whatever is given to them (Luke 10:8). The only "agenda" they have is to heal the sick and let people know the kingdom of God had come near.

Referring to this passage, Clemens Sedmak, in *Doing Local Theology*, states that Jesus taught his disciples that "they should not arrive with ready-made tools and concepts [when entering a town]; instead they should first assess the situation and accept the local quality of life."[2] In the same way, VCG participants engage their vocational activities without the drive to achieve any particular goal other than to simply know their neighbors through listening.

When God's people go out with no agenda, they are able to remain open to seeing people as people, rather than as *objects* of ministry, and to see the ways God might already be at work in their lives. This openness helps them to participate in their vocational activity with a posture of learning. And when we come genuinely ready to learn, that lowers peoples' defenses in return and breeds a spirit of openness and acceptance.

In order to discover the fresh calling of God, not only for each person individually, but also for the church they are a part of, VCG participants need to be open to whatever God might reveal. And in order to be open to what God reveals, we need to drop our agendas.

Really Listening Really Matters

Okay, here comes a really bad joke. Ready?

> *My boss yelled at me today saying, "You weren't even listening just now, were you?" I thought to myself, "Man, what a weird way to start a conversation..."*

Listening can be really hard, can't it? We can get so caught up in our own thoughts or get so focused on what we're doing that we don't even notice when someone is speaking to us.

But not listening can be a lot more subtle than unintentionally (or intentionally) ignoring someone. There are times when we might be deep in conversation with a person, yet not really be listening to them. We fail (or perhaps *refuse*) to truly hear what they are trying to communicate. This often happens when we are arguing with someone. At those times, we're not really listening to what our conversation partner is saying. All we're thinking about is what we're going to say next to counter their argument.

There are, of course, times when perhaps we shouldn't listen. When a toxic relationship, for instance, is filled with cutting remarks and verbal abuse, it's best not to listen.

But when it comes to participating with God in his mission in the world, we have to listen. If we're going to join God in bringing healing and wholeness to the world, we have to listen to God and we have to listen to our neighbors. This is a matter of good theology, believe it or not!

Discerning what God is up to in the world involves an intentional process of action and reflection. A Vocational Connection Group helps church members get involved in their vocational activities—in their jobs, in their neighborhoods, in their families, and so forth—and pay attention to what God is doing in and through the lives of those with whom they interact.

When attending their vocational activity, the task of the Vocational Connection Group participants is to listen to what others are saying. And how exactly do they go about listening? Simply by engaging in casual conversation with others—by asking good questions and by listening for what people may be struggling with, what they are looking forward to, where they feel energy in their lives, and so forth.

Listening is critical for the Vocational Connection Group process. It helps them understand their neighbors and it helps them become aware of God's activity in the world. In this sense, listening is a key practice of good theology. Clemens Sedmak writes, "It is not so much the ability to talk but the abilities to listen and observe that make a good theologian."[3] Theology, in other words, is at its best when the theologian pays attention to what is *actually* going on in the world and then makes connections to God and to the Scriptures. In this way, "theology is simply a mindfulness of God, and attentiveness to the action of God in creation."[4]

Here's what I'm saying: the VCG participants, through

the mere act of listening to and observing their neighbors in the context of their vocations, are doing theology. By paying attention to what is going on around them in their neighborhoods, in their workplaces, in their families, they are becoming theologians in that they are becoming more aware of what God is doing in the world and how their local church might join in God's mission.

VCG participants do "local theology" by accessing "local theological resources,"[5] as Sedmak puts it. They are doing what Sedmak says the followers of Jesus must do—they "have to leave their desk and go out among the people to listen to their songs and jokes, to see their daily life and their struggle to survive and to sustain their dependents."[6]

You see, as we *listen* to the "songs and jokes" and recognize the "struggle to survive" of those with whom we connect in our vocational activities, we discover what God is up to in the world. And that's what we call doing theology.

Thingification

The reason doing theology is so important is because it keeps us focused on what really matters to God—people. Unfortunately, sometimes when a church engages in ministry, it can forget about the people.

Don't get me wrong. I love the church. I've heard it said that the church is the hope of the world—and I agree! The church is the Body of Christ and the light of the world. I firmly believe that it is through the church that God will bring healing and redemption to the brokenness of the world.

And so we celebrate with joy churches that are growing as people in their communities come to faith in Jesus. We rejoice in the many ministries of healing and restoration that churches provide through which people find wholeness for their lives. Churches provide many wonderful ministries that do lots of good in people's lives.

And, yet, we have to acknowledge that one of the greatest dangers of church ministry is that, under the pressure to grow our churches or produce results, we run the risk of forgetting that people are *people*, not mere *consumers* of spiritual goods and services. The people we serve each have their own stories. Each person has their own struggles, their own joys, their own hopes, their own fears.

I can be guilty of this. I sometimes forget that the people in my congregation don't exist just to make my church look good. I sometimes forget that they don't exist simply to invite other people to church, or to serve as an usher, or to volunteer for Vacation Bible School.

The people in my congregation are not gears in the church machine.

And what about the people outside my church? How do I view them? Sometimes I am guilty of viewing people outside my church as objects, too. Not always, but sometimes.

Sometimes—in my mind—the people in our neighborhood exist for the sake of sending their kids to our preschool. Or they exist in order to attend our Christmas program. Or they exist to be a part of our Community Garden. Or they exist in order to hopefully start going to our church so our church would have higher attendance and a bigger budget. Unfortunately, though intentions are almost always good, it's not unusual for a ministry strategy to objectify people by viewing them as little more than consumers of the latest church plan or ministry program.

Thomas H. Groome, in *Sharing Faith*, calls this approach

to ministry "thingification."[7] "Thingification" is the objectification of human beings, thinking of them more as objects than as people. It is the refusal, as Groome puts it, to "treat some people as persons."[8] "Thingification" is what happens when people don't listen to one another. (And there's a lot of *not listening* in the world today, isn't there?)

So what's the cure for "thingification"? Well, if "thingification" is what happens when we *don't* listen, then the cure must be listening. When we listen—really listen—to the people in our congregations, to the people in our neighborhoods, to the people in our workplaces, it becomes much more difficult to objectify those people.

Listening forces us to understand others as real people rather than as objects—as things—whose purpose is to consume whatever the church's latest spiritual "product" happens to be. As we learn to listen and know the people in our churches and communities, that's when we will begin to get a sense of how God might be calling us to join him in the work of healing the world. A Vocational Connection Group is designed to foster this kind of listening.

Reflection

Action—which, in Vocational Connection Groups consists of engaging with and listening to people in one's vocational spheres—is the first component of discerning what God is already doing in the world and how we might participate with God. The other major component of the Vocational Connection Group process is reflection. Action is good and important, but "action is not completed until it has been reflected upon."[9] Reflection involves essentially two components: sharing and listening.

1. *Sharing:* Group members share with one another stories of what they experienced in their places of vocation. Who did they talk with? What did they talk about? What stories did they hear? What do they think God might be up to?
2. *Listening:* As each group member shares, the others listen. But they don't listen only to one another, they also listen to God through Scripture and prayer.

Monthly Reflection Meetings

It is important for reflection times to happen on a regular basis. At least once a month, all VCG participants gather together to reflect on what they sensed God doing in their vocational activities. This is done by spending some time in the Scriptures, by sharing and listening to what everyone experienced in their vocational engagement, and by praying together for their neighborhood, for their workplaces, for their schools, and so forth.

One of the reasons for holding a monthly reflection meeting is to help form a people who are ever more aware of God's activity in and around them. This involves learning. One of the key learnings that needs to take place for VCG participants is a kind of paradigm shift—a shift from belief that ministry is initiated with church activities and programs toward a belief and understanding that ministry begins wherever God's people live their lives.

Another purpose for reflection meetings is to form people in such a way that they begin to view the world through a missional lens. This happens simply by connecting with others who are also on mission with God. Monthly reflection meetings create a space in which people can share what they have seen God doing in the world as they look at the Scriptures together, as they share stories of what they experienced in their vocational engagement, and as they pray together for the people and networks in their vocational spheres.

What a Reflection Meeting Looks Like

Each monthly reflection meeting consists of four parts.

1. *Dwelling in Scripture.* The VCG participants begin the meeting by spending time reading and reflecting on God's Word together, listening for how God may be speaking to them at this particular time and in this particular place.
2. *Sharing stories.* The bulk of the reflection meeting is spent sharing stories, insights, and questions based on their experiences in their vocational activities over the course of the past month.
3. *Prayer.* Finally, the group closes with a time of prayer for the people in their neighborhoods and vocational spheres, for their church, and for any other concerns that may have come up during the reflection time.

If you're counting, you'll notice that I only gave you three parts of the reflection meeting—even though I said there are four parts. What's missing?

There is a fourth component that runs through the entire reflection meeting—and, really, through the entire Vocational Connection Group process. The fourth aspect of the monthly reflection meeting can be summed up in one word.

4. *Openness.*

This fourth component—*openness*—involves discovering how God is active in the places where the participants are engaging their neighbors, perhaps *even in unexpected ways.* All four components are essential to discovering what God is up to and how God might be inviting the church to join him in what he is doing in the world.

Dwelling in Scripture

Each reflection meeting begins with a time of dwelling in Scripture. It is a period of time at the beginning of the meeting during which the group reads and reflects on a passage of Scripture. This opening time is meant to help participants begin to tune in to what God might want to say to the group that day. It also reminds the group that the stories they are about to share and hear are part of a bigger story—God's big story that has been going on since the beginning of time (and even before that!).

Dwelling in Scripture as a group consists of three stages:

1. Read the text together.
2. Spend about a minute in silence to review the text and reflect on where the text connected with each person or what questions or ideas were raised for them personally.
3. Turn back to the group and share their reflections on the passage of Scripture.

The Purpose of Dwelling in Scripture

Dwelling in Scripture helps the group members connect with God's Word in a deep and meaningful way in light of what is actually going on in their lives. It allows them to see their own lives, including their neighborhood and vocational engagement, as part of a larger story with a greater purpose. The objective of dwelling in Scripture is not to try to figure out what the text means. Rather, the purpose is to discover how the text connects with each person on that day and, by extension, how the text relates to the group as a whole.

To be clear, dwelling in Scripture is not an exegetical exercise. It is not meant to unearth the original meaning of the text or the exact implications of the original Greek or Hebrew. Dwelling in Scripture is more like *lectio divina*, a kind of reading that immerses the reader in the text. It is more like entering into relationship with the text or becoming a character in the text. It is less about what God was saying to the original audience and more about what God is saying to this audience.

This does not, however, give license to misinterpret the passage. Any gross misinterpretation should be corrected by the group. But dwelling in Scripture does make room for God to say something to *this person* and *this group* at *this time* and in *this place*. It involves an openness to the presence and activity of God here and now. As the group listens to God through the text, they prepare their hearts and minds to discover God at work in the world.

Use the Same Text Every Time

I recommend that the group dwell in the same passage of Scripture every time they meet. If that sounds too limiting, I suggest that, at the very least, the group stay with a particular passage three or four times in a row before moving on to a new text. The purpose of this is to allow the text to speak ever more deeply to each of the participants, as well as to the whole group, with each passing month. Staying with the same text is the essence of dwelling in Scripture. It allows the group to become familiar with that particular Scripture and invites God to speak over time in new ways through a single biblical passage.

You may experience the temptation to read a different text each time the VCG meets. Some participants may even push back on repeatedly sticking with a single passage. They may express impatience or frustration. You will need to use your own judgment as you respond to this feedback. But I urge you to encourage your people to try to stick with a single passage for at least several months.

While studying a different text at each reflection meeting might give participants a broader overview of the Scriptures, dwelling in the same text repeatedly allows that text to reach into each person's life just a little bit more each time and makes it more likely for that Scripture to stay with them the next time they engage their vocational activity.

Suggested Passages for Dwelling in Scripture

The specific text that is used for dwelling in Scripture is not critical, though certain texts do lend themselves more readily to reflecting on God's mission in the world and our place in it. Here are several texts I would recommend:

- *Genesis 12:1-8.* God sends Abraham to a new land and promises that he and his descendants will be a blessing to the world.
- *Exodus 2:23-3:10.* God calls Moses to embrace a challenging mission.
- *Jeremiah 29:1-14.* Jeremiah writes to the exiles in Babylon, inviting them to settle down in their place of exile and pray for the shalom of the city.
- *Luke 10:1-11.* Jesus sends out the seventy-two disciples to go into nearby towns, stay there, and announce the Kingdom of God.
- *Acts 1:1-10.* After promising the Holy Spirit and charging them to be his witnesses, Jesus is taken up into heaven.
- *Acts 2:37-47.* The early church grows and experiments with a countercultural way of life.
- *Romans 12:1-21.* Paul paints a picture of what a transformed life looks like, especially in regard to one's neighbors.
- *Ephesians 4:11-16.* Paul describes various roles in the church and what a spiritually mature congregation looks like.

One final thought. While one of the greatest values of dwelling in Scripture is the practice of remaining with a single text for an extended season of time so that the text saturates the hearts of the group members, you may find value in reading a different translation of the text each time your Vocational Connection Group meets. The various translations can draw out different nuances of the text, which can lead to deep discovery by the group.

Sharing Stories

After closing the time of dwelling in Scripture with a short prayer, the group moves into a period of sharing, discussion, and reflection. During this part of the meeting, participants exchange stories of what they heard and experienced in their vocational activities that month. They share about the people they encountered, conversations they had, and observations they made. At the same time, they have an opportunity to listen to other participants share about the experiences they have had over the past month.

This time of sharing creates the space needed to begin discovering what God might be doing in their various vocational spheres. It is important for each person to share their experiences and thoughts. Through mutual openness and contemplation, each person can make new observations and discover deeper insights about their experiences. Thomas H. Groome, in *Sharing Faith*, says that a person learns as they seek to "foster dialogue and conversation with oneself, with others, and with God."[10] This "dialogue and conversation" occurs as group members share their experiences, and it is by sharing their experiences that God's activity begins to become evident. This is a critical first step to eventually discovering the mission to which God may be calling both individual members of the group and even the congregation as a whole.

Mutual Learning

This time of sharing also fosters mutual learning among the group members that leads to a unity of mind and spirit. Such mutual learning and growing unity emerges through the dialogue that takes place in the reflection meetings.

"Dialogue with others," says Groome, "is an honest sharing of one's own story/vision and an empathetic listening to their word and expressions in true conversation."[11]

Discovering what God is doing and how God might be calling the people of God can only be accomplished through such "honest sharing," "empathetic listening," and "true conversation." The more the group meets, shares, listens, and affirms one another, the more they will trust one another and feel united with one another. When this kind of deep dialogue takes place, Groome says, it "is an event of mutual discovery and discernment."[12] It is a kind of coming together, not only of ideas about what God is up to in the world, but also a unifying of hearts as they converge for the purpose of joining God in his mission.

The Transformative Power of Sharing Stories

The kind of learning cultivated in the reflection meetings is intended not only to bring up information and insight into how God is active in the participants' vocational spheres, but also to help participants begin to change the way they think about where and how ministry begins. The common wisdom in churches has been that ministry begins with the "professional" Christians (e.g., the pastors and staff). Many church members assume that it is the church staff's job to come up with a strategic plan for the church. The strategic plan leads to the formation of ministry programs and an invitation to the congregation to get involved in the programs. If church members are convinced that the ministry programs are worth their time and effort, they may offer some of their leisure time to engage in the ministry programs initiated by the church staff.

This paradigm—rooted in a Christendom mentality—

assumes that ministry starts with the "professional" Christians and trickles down to the "ordinary" Christians. It is an assumption that, unfortunately, keeps the church from being all that God intends the church to be.

This paradigm of ministry needs to change. And change is hard.

But... Change becomes possible as VCG participants share and listen to one another's stories. Paradigms begin to shift in people's minds as they engage in conversation with one another. An inner transformation begins to take place.

Conversation is critical in fostering such change, because, as Pascale, Milleman, and Gioja state in *Surfing the Edge of Chaos*, "conversation is the single most important business process when the goal is to shift what people believe and how they think."[13] While Vocational Connection Groups aren't a "business," per se, the principle holds: conversation allows people to be part of the transformation process. To put it even more strikingly, "conversation is the source and soul of change."[14]

As Vocational Connection Group members engage in conversation with one another (and with their neighbors in their vocational spheres), they begin to discover that ministry actually begins with them. Ministry begins when they become aware of where God is at work around them and then get involved in what God is doing.

But that's a big change. And for someone to embrace a big change like that, they have to be given the opportunity to process the change. They need the space to reflect on why change is necessary, what options are available, how they might be personally affected by change, and other implications of change. That's why regular time for reflection is so important to the Vocational Connection Group process. With room to reflect, group members' understanding of where and how ministry starts can be transformed.

Asking Questions

Asking thoughtful and incisive questions is a key component of effective reflection. In regard to the learning and discovery process, Michael Marquardt writes, "Questions will always be more powerful than statements...."[15] This is because asking questions, first of all, helps a group to better understand the challenge before them and, second, draws the group's attention toward possible solutions.

The power of asking questions lies in the ability to "create the space for something new to emerge."[16] Questions open the group up to new possibilities. They allow the group "to recognize and reorganize their knowledge."[17] By recognizing their assumption about where and how ministry begins and reorganizing their knowledge about God, the church, themselves, the world, and their vocations, group members can position themselves to more readily accept that God is calling them to participate in God's mission in the seemingly mundane and ordinary places of their lives—the places where they work, eat, sleep, and play.

Questions are absolutely necessary for deep learning to take place. Marquardt puts it this way: "Deep and significant learning occurs only as a result of reflection and reflection is not possible without a question."[18] Basic learning can take place in various ways—through lectures, by reading, by watching educational documentaries, or by experiencing something firsthand.

To engage a deeper level of learning, however, questions need to be asked. "Why did this happen?" "What does this mean?" "How did things get to this point?" and other such probing questions elicit a kind of critical reflection that otherwise wouldn't occur. It is, therefore, the Vocational Connection Group facilitator's job to ask effective questions (though group members will likely also ask good questions as the reflection meetings progress).

Sample Questions

What questions should be asked to help the group think more deeply about the actions they have taken in their vocational activities? What questions can help group members consider the connection between the people they have interacted with, their own gifts and skills, God's desire for the world, and the resources and gifts that their congregation can bring to bear on a given situation?

Here is a list of questions that can be asked during a reflection meeting:

- Did you meet or talk with anyone new?
- What stories did you hear?
- What surprised you in your conversations?
- What is God up to in your vocational locale?
- How might God be calling you to join him in what he is doing?
- How might God be calling our church to join him in what he is doing?
- How did you do at listening to people?
- Did you have to step out of your comfort zone?
- How were you stretched?
- Can you connect anything that has been shared today to the Scripture we read at the beginning of the meeting?

- Did anything excite you in your vocational sphere this past month? Did anything upset you?
- What do you think causes the challenges you heard people share about this past month?
- What are people in your vocational sphere excited about? Anxious about? Angry about?
- Could you say more about...[a thought or topic they already mentioned]?
- Where did you see life and energy in your vocational activities? What seemed to excite people?
- Do you see any themes beginning to appear in your vocational sphere?
- Do we as a group see any themes emerging across all our experiences?

This is not, of course, an exhaustive list of questions. As you think of new helpful questions be sure to write them down so you can ask them the next time you meet.

Prayer

Each reflection meeting is closed with a time of prayer. This accomplishes two things. First, closing the reflection time by praying together serves as a reminder that God is involved both in their vocational activities and in their reflection time together. Second, the people's prayers invite God to become further involved in the places of their vocations (cf. 2 Chronicles 7:14).

Prayer is a reminder that God is present (cf. Deuteronomy 31:8; Philippians 4:6-7). Prayer reminds us that human beings and human activity are a part of something much bigger. "Prayer," writes Parker J. Palmer, "is our capacity to enter into the vast community of life in which self and other, human and nonhuman, visible and invisible, are intricately intertwined."[19] Prayer, in other words, is more than merely talking to God; it is a means by which God connects us to the needs, the hopes, and the joys of the world and the people around us.

In prayer, we acknowledge and learn that there is a "transcendent center that connects it all."[20] When we pray, God, who is the "transcendent center," joins us to our loved ones, to our neighbors, and even to our enemies in a way that ultimately brings healing and wholeness to ourselves and to the world. By closing each reflection meeting with a time of prayer, VCG participants remember that God, "the transcendent center," is at work both in their vocational engagement and in their time of dialogue and reflection.

Prayer also invites God to become further involved in their neighborhoods, in their vocational spheres, and in the group's own learning and growth. While we don't have time here to explore exactly how prayer works, the Scriptures seem to indicate that prayer has an effect on God's action (check out Genesis 18:20-33, Exodus 33:12-23, James 5:16). By closing the reflection meetings with prayer, the group asks and expects that God will continue to be active in and through their various vocations, bringing the healing and wholeness for which they pray.

Openness to the Unexpected

Dwelling in Scripture, sharing stories and experiences, and praying together are the three primary components of the reflection meetings. Woven throughout these three is a fourth component. This fourth component, as mentioned above, is an *openness* to discovering what God is doing in one's vocational sphere and how God's people might participate with God regardless of prior expectations.

Openness is critical for us to perceive new and unexpected possibilities. Human tendency is to try to find a solution to a problem as quickly as possible, using whatever knowledge and means are currently at our disposal. Peter Block points out that human beings "believe that defining, analyzing, and studying problems is the way to make a better world."[21] He immediately adds, however, that this problem-solving approach "may actually limit any chance of the future being different from the past."[22]

In order for a church to discover a new future, to move past that which might even be getting in the way of how God is calling them to minister, a church must step beyond mere problem-solving into an openness that allows for something new to emerge. With such new ideas, new insights, new relationships, and even new questions, a church can move into a future that may be completely unexpected.

Churches are prone to try to find solutions to problems as quickly as possible. Marquardt says, "understanding the problem is the most important step in problem solving.... Yet most individuals and groups rush into the search for the answers."[23] Rather than rush to a solution, the Vocational Connection Group process "forces the group to spend time on understanding the problem and its context and conditions."[24]

Whereas human tendency, when faced with a missional challenge or problem, is to hurry toward a solution, the process of intentional action and measured reflection is designed to allow new possibilities to emerge as participants slow down to reflect on what they are learning and experiencing.

How does a church cultivate an openness toward the unexpected? I would suggest that there are two ways this happens. The first is through the practice of asking effective questions. The process of asking questions, in other words, "creates the physiological and psychological conditions for learning and thus augments learning opportunities."[25] In a sense, by asking the kinds of questions that generate openness to the unexpected, the group can allow the solutions to find them. Palmer says, "Truth is constantly seeking us."[26] By resisting the urge to rush to an answer, those who engage in reflection "open a space in which truth might find us out."[27] It is in the openness to the unexpected that one eventually finds the answer.

The second way the Vocational Connection Group can lean into an openness to the unexpected is through surrender. Discerning God's will and following where God's will leads requires that we let go of our own desires, our own will, our own expectations. This is why dwelling in Scripture and prayer are so important. They are the spiritual practices that help us move toward surrender. It is only as we surrender more and more to God that we are truly able to be open to wherever and however God leads us.

It is my hope that in the openness to the unexpected your church will begin to think in new ways about where and how ministry begins. My desire is that your church would discover that ministry doesn't begin with a brainstorming session of staff and elders or through the latest church program or initiative. Rather, may your people discover that ministry begins where they already are engaged in their neighborhoods and their vocations.

God is already there. Will you be open to joining God where he is already at work?

6

PLANNING AND PURPOSE

(OR HOW TO IMPLEMENT VOCATIONAL CONNECTION GROUPS)

One of my favorite movie scenes is from the 2002 movie, *Spider-Man* (the one with Tobey Maguire and, in my opinion, the best of the many *Spider-Man* movies!). Having been bitten by a spider while on a school field trip near the beginning of the movie, Peter Parker crashes into bed feeling terrible at the end of the day. Little does he know that the spider that bit him had been a genetically enhanced spider—and his life is about to change!

When Peter wakes up, he puts his glasses on just like he does every morning. But something is wrong—with his glasses on, everything is blurry. When he takes them off, he can see perfectly. "Weird," Peter mumbles.

That's when he notices something else. He looks at himself in the mirror and notices that he is *ripped!* He's utterly confused—and totally stoked! When he crashed into bed the night before, he had been a scrawny, skinny kid. This morning Peter is all muscle!

You know why I love that scene? Because I would *love* for

that to happen to me! I wish I would just wake up one day and—without warning—be in the best shape of my life.

Be honest. You totally wish that would happen to you, too. And maybe it will!

Or maybe not...

The reality is, if you're going to get in shape, it's going to take a lot of energy and effort. But that's how it is with just about anything that's worth doing.

Learning to read in Kindergarten takes practice. Earning a college degree takes work. Starting a business requires effort. No one ever wakes up one day knowing how to read or having earned a college degree or having started a successful business.

In the same way, discerning God's activity in the world so we can join him in what he is doing doesn't "just happen." We need to work at paying attention. We need to engage our neighbors and neighborhoods with intentionality. We need to purposefully pray and listen to God. We live in a Post-Christendom world and simply doing what we've always done will not help God's people become who they were meant to be. And it won't help the world become what God longs for the world to be.

I say all this because it will take some effort to implement a Vocational Connection Group in your church. It will take planning and purpose to make a Vocational Connection Group happen.

That's why I want to lay out the process of implementing a Vocational Connection Group as clearly and simply as I can. I want to take out as much of the guesswork as possible so that you can get to the work of discernment as soon as possible. The whole process can be boiled down to three phases:

1. Lay the Groundwork.
2. Engage in Action-Reflection
3. Choose an Experiment

And that's about it. In the remainder of this chapter, I'll unpack what is involved in each of these three phases.

PHASE 1: LAY THE GROUNDWORK

For the Vocational Connection Group to be effective, it's important to get started the right way. Otherwise, you'll lose people before you even begin. You may face resistance from other leaders. You may be asked tough questions about why the church should do a VCG. You might even be tempted to give up yourself if you don't lay the groundwork properly.

In this phase, you will need to intentionally decide to do a VCG. You'll need to get buy-in from the leadership of the church, both staff and lay leadership. You'll have to make decisions about when to start and who to invite to be a part of the VCG.

Decide To Do It

The first step in Phase 1 of the Vocational Connection Group process is to simply *decide* that you are going to *do it.* Decide that the church can't go on living with the sacred/secular divide that keeps the majority of God's people from participating in God's mission. Decide that, more than providing spiritual goods and services, your church needs to join God in God's mission in the world. Decide that discerning God's call for your church and for the people within your church is worth the effort. Decide that you will give the energy required to implement a Vocational Connection Group.

Get Buy-in From Leadership

Once you've decided to conduct a Vocational Connection Group you will need to present the idea to your leadership team. You will need their buy-in in order to get the most out of your Vocational Connection Group. The leadership team —whether it's a staff team, a board of elders or deacons, or other top-level group of decision makers—needs to understand the purpose of the Vocational Connection Group and offer their support.

Top-level leadership teams can be very protective of existing programs or resistant to anything that feels like "rocking the boat." That's why it is so important for them to know that you will *not* be starting a new ministry program. The Vocational Connection Group is not designed to replace anything the church is currently doing. It is meant to help God's people discern where and how God is at work in the world, with the expectation that God will reveal new ways for the church to join him in his mission. Thus, these are the things the leadership team needs to know:

1. You will be leading a handful of church members through a process of listening to God, listening to their neighbors, and listening to one another in order to discern where God may be calling them to participate with God in his mission in the world.
2. This will be a process of spiritual formation for the VCG participants, leading to deeper relationships with God and with one another.

3. The group will together decide on an experiment —a small-scale, prototype ministry designed to help people participate in what God is doing in their community.
4. The hope is to discern new ways for the church to get involved in God's work in the world.

The leadership team—if they see the value of conducting a Vocational Connection Group—will need to give two things to the Vocational Connection Group participants: *permission* and *authority*.

Permission is not too hard to come by. Most leadership teams are happy to allow church members to try something new—as long as it doesn't interfere with existing programs.

But the VCG needs more than just permission. It also needs authority. It needs to be given the authority to try new things—new ways of connecting with neighbors, new ways of blessing neighbors, new experimental ministries.

This is why the language of experimentation is so important. As long as the VCG's activities are *experiments*, leadership teams will feel less resistant to granting authority to try new things. The language of experimentation also allows for failure—perhaps the ministry experiment will be a complete flop. If that happens—and prototypes, by the way, are supposed to fail—that's totally okay because failing is a learning experience. If the experiment fails, the team will have learned from experience something that *won't* work. The reality is that a few ministry experiments will likely need to fail before the right ministry is discovered.

In order to conduct ministry experiments, the VCG participants need to have the freedom to try new things. Marquardt, in *Optimizing the Power of Action Learning* (the VCG process is a variation of the "action learning" process), says that in order to effectively solve a problem the group must be "given the authority and power to solve [the problem] and to implement action."[1] (In the VCG process, the "problem" can be summarized as the church's lack of awareness of how God is inviting them to join the mission of God). The VCG needs authority to experiment because "if the group has been notified that it is merely to make recommendations, which may or may not be implemented, the group's energy level will be low, members will be less creative, frustration and/or apathy may arise, and members may skip meetings and not undertake agreed-upon tasks."[2]

When the church's top leadership team buys into the VCG process and gives to the VCG the authority to try out ministry experiments, the Vocational Connection Group has the greatest chance of discovering how God is inviting the church to participate with him in his mission.

Decide When to Start

Put a start date and an end date on the calendar. When will you hold your first reflection meeting with the Vocational Connection Group participants? When will you hold the final reflection retreat? Will you follow the calendar year (January through December) or the school year (September through June)? Once you have set the start date, you can work backwards to determine when to announce the VCG to the congregation and invite people personally to participate. Locking in a start date is also helpful because it provides a deadline for recruitment—and deadlines can be very effective motivators!

Identify Potential Participants

The most effective way to recruit participants is to identify which congregation members you think would be most beneficial to the group and who might benefit most from participating. Think about people in your congregation who are relatively mature in their faith and who care about their community.

The group should ultimately have about 6-10 people. To get those 6-10 people, start by making a list of at least thirty people who might be a good fit for the Vocational Connection Group. Some of those thirty will naturally decline the invitation. Odds are you'll find enough who will say yes—and you'll have your group of 6-10 VCG participants.

As you compile your list of thirty people, it would also be wise to include some staff and lay leaders from your board or session. You will need some who are in leadership in order for the learning and discerning to spread to other leaders and eventually throughout the congregation.

Invite People Personally

Once you've made your list of thirty people, start inviting them personally. Take them out to coffee. Buy them lunch. Share your passion for participating with God in what God is up to in the world. Explain what the VCG is designed to accomplish and how they can be a part of the new ways God wants to begin to work through your church.

Be sure to give them the logistical details. Tell them when the VCG will start and when you'll need to have their decision. Let them know what they are committing to:

1. They will need to engage regularly in a neighborhood or vocational activity (though it may be something they are already doing).
2. They will need to attend a monthly reflection meeting.
3. They will need to be open to discovering unexpected ways that God wants to work through them to bring healing and wholeness to the world.

Announce to the Congregation

It is also wise to announce the Vocational Connection Group to the whole congregation. It's a good idea to do this for a few reasons:

1. *It's a teaching opportunity.* You can help the congregation see that we live in a new era in which doing what we've always done isn't working anymore. We need to discover the new things God is doing in the world so that we can be a part of what God is up to.
2. *It helps the congregation feel in the loop.* Many congregation members won't want to participate in a Vocational Connection Group—at least not immediately. For many it may seem like just another item to put on the calendar. But knowing about the VCG gives them a sense of connection and ownership in the VCG. And the next time they are invited they may say yes!
3. *God may lead you to some VCG participants you hadn't considered.* Don't forget that only God is omniscient. There may be someone in your

> congregation who is totally ready, both emotionally and spiritually, to engage in the Vocational Connection Group—but it may never have crossed your mind to invite them. God may have been at work in this person in ways no one else knows about, and they may be exactly the right person for the VCG. Be open to the unexpected!

Be sure to have a process for signing up, whether it's a sign-up sheet in the lobby or Narthex, a card they can drop in the offering, or an online sign-up form on the church website. You may also want to hold a 45-minute informational meeting after church for anyone interested in participating.

What if you end up with twenty or thirty people who want to participate? That, of course, is too many people for one group. You can't have deep conversation with more than ten or twelve participants. If you have lots of people interested, you'll have to decide if you want to conduct two or more separate groups at the same time, or if you want to invite people to join a VCG the next time around.

PHASE 2: ENGAGE IN ACTION-REFLECTION

Phase 2 is the meat of the Vocational Connection Group process. This is where participants engage in their vocational activities and come together to reflect on what they experienced. This is where new ideas begin to emerge and new ways of thinking begin to percolate. This is where the group learns to listen to their neighbors, to each other, and to God.

Let's unpack what is involved in Phase 2 of the VCG process.

Conduct the First Reflection Meeting

Now it begins!

You set the date for your first reflection meeting several months ago. Today is the day for that meeting! This is your first official gathering of the Vocational Connection Group and the first time you'll be engaging in a time of intentional reflection.

After thanking the participants for volunteering to be a part of this process, open the reflection meeting with prayer. After the prayer, take a few minutes to describe what you'll be doing in this reflection meeting. Help them understand the following components of the meeting:

- *Dwelling in Scripture.* Let them know which passage of scripture you'll be spending time in during your reflection meetings and why you'll be staying in a single passage throughout the process. Help the group understand that this is a time for listening to God through his Word so they can listen well when they are in their vocational activities. It's about spiritual formation.
- *Sharing stories.* This will be a time of sharing what each person experienced in their vocational activities during the previous month. Inform them that they need to listen to one another so that they can hear what God might be saying to the group. It's also a time for noticing themes that

emerge in their stories so that they can develop a ministry experiment by the fifth or sixth reflection meeting.
- *Prayer.* Remind the group that as they close their reflection meeting in prayer they are growing in awareness of God's involvement and presence in their vocational activities and they are inviting God to become further involved in the life of their community and the lives of the people with whom they interact. This time of prayer is also a time of surrendering to the ways in which God might call this congregation to join him in his mission.

Once you've informed the group of the reflection meeting structure, work through each component of the meeting. Start by spending twenty minutes dwelling in scripture. Read the selected passage, give them a few moments of silence to reflect personally on the passage, and then come together to share what struck each person and how they sense God speaking to them through the text.

Next, enter into a period of sharing stories. At this first reflection meeting, the group won't have yet intentionally engaged in their vocational activities, so they won't yet have any stories to share from their vocational activities. However, they can share their own stories. So, in this first meeting, use this time for introductions. Have each person share:

- Their name.
- A little bit about their family.
- Where did they grow up?

- A summary of their faith journey. How did they first learn about Jesus? When did their faith become real for them? What challenges have they encountered along their faith journey? How has God been faithful to them?
- A little bit about their experience in the church. What drew them to this church? How long have they been there? What are some hopes they have for their church?
- Why did they volunteer to participate in the Vocational Connection Group?
- What will their vocational activity be over the course of the Vocational Connection Group and why did they choose that activity?

Finally, close the meeting with ten minutes of group prayer. Pray for each of the members of the group and for the vocational activities in which they will be engaging. Ask God to use the months that follow to reveal to them the ways in which God is already active in the lives of people in their community and the ways that God is inviting his people to join him.

Engage in Vocational Activities

Between the first reflection meeting and the next one, VCG participants will begin the work of connecting with and listening to their neighbors in their vocational activities. They will intentionally have conversations with colleagues, fellow parents, fellow retirees, fellow students, neighbors, and so forth, paying purposeful attention to their hopes and joys, their fears and anxieties, and even the seemingly mundane aspects of their everyday lives.

It is as they pay attention to their neighbors that they begin to love their neighbors more deeply. And it is by listening to their neighbors that they begin to get a sense of what God is up to in the world.

Next Reflection Meeting

About one month after the first reflection meeting, the group will gather for their second reflection meeting. They will again spend time dwelling in scripture. They will again share stories, only this time they will have stories of neighborhood and vocational engagement to tell. They will begin to share stories that indicate what God is up to in their vocational spheres. Finally, they will again pray together to invite God into their lives and vocational activities, and pray that they would discern how God is inviting them to join him in his mission.

Continue the Action-Reflection Cycle

From here on, the process of action and reflection repeats over and over again. The participants engage their neighbors in their vocational activities, engage God's Word in the scriptures and prayer, and engage one another as they share their stories. As the team moves through each cycle of action and reflection, they learn just a little bit more, discerning just a little more fully what God is up to in the world.

Track Emerging Themes

One of the challenges of the action-reflection process will be to pay attention to the themes that emerge over the course of the process. It will be especially important to *not forget* what themes come to light.

Here's what I mean. During some reflection meetings, the group may be captivated by a particular story, which will lead to another story, which will lead to a profound thought or idea. That's great! The following month, the group may be struck by a completely different story and all but forget about what had captured their imagination at the previous meeting.

Because of this, it will be important to *designate someone to take notes for the group*. They should take notes both during the time of dwelling in scripture and the time of sharing stories. It is during these times of reflection and sharing that themes of God's activity and invitation will emerge.

After each reflection meeting, the facilitator should take the notes, type them up, and review them prior to the following reflection meeting. He or she should be ever mindful of all the ways God is speaking to and through the group so that the group can best discern how God is inviting them to participate in God's mission.

Mid-point Reflection Retreat

After the group has been meeting and reflecting together for five or six months, it is time for the group to start thinking about a ministry experiment. This is not yet the final ministry experiment (which is Phase 3 of the VCG process) and it does not need to be a complicated ministry experiment, but it should be something that the whole group agrees to and commits to. It could be as simple as going for walks in the neighborhood together to pray for their neighbors. It could be to serve at the local homeless shelter once a week. It could be to invite a local expert on immigration to speak at a community event hosted by the church.

Why is it important for the group to choose a ministry experiment halfway through the Vocational Connection Group process? Because *doing something* is incredibly formational. In order to learn as much as possible, and to take a step of deeper involvement with God in the world, they will need to spend several months reflecting on what they are discovering through a simple ministry experiment.

Keep in mind that the purpose of this ministry experiment is simply to *try something*—to take action—and then reflect on what God may be saying to the group in light of the ministry experiment. The group should reflect together on questions like:

- Is the ministry experiment effective? How do we measure effectiveness?
- Is the experiment a formative experience for participants? In what ways? How does this ministry experiment help them grow in their faith? How is it helping them become more like Jesus?
- Does it help them discern God's activity in the world?
- Do they sense God's leading as they engage in the ministry experiment?
- What kind of feedback are they receiving from those they are serving?

It is important for the group to be brutally honest as

they ask these questions. It's not unusual to want to spin the outcome of a project in a positive way, especially if the project was our idea. Don't do that! If the ministry experiment isn't particularly effective, say so. If it isn't spiritually formative for participants, be honest about that. And, of course, if it does seem to be effective, discuss and discover why that is. What is God up to through this ministry experiment? Which doors is God opening? Which doors is God closing?

So, if the experiment turns out to be a great success, fantastic! But, if it ends up as an apparent failure, that's also good! It means that the group has learned something. The fact is, this experiment should probably not be a wild success. It should, however—through the action-reflection process—help the group get a better sense of what God is or is not up to and how God may be calling them to join him.

At the end of the VCG process, the group will have another opportunity to imagine a new ministry experiment, based not only on what they learned from this first experiment, but also on a full ten to twelve months of vocational action and reflection.

Continued Reflection Meetings

In the second half of the Vocational Connection Group process (after the mid-point reflection retreat), participants will continue to engage their vocational activities. They will continue to listen to the people in their vocational spheres, pay attention to what God might be doing in their lives, and then share with the VCG what they observed and experienced.

During this time, the group will also engage in the

ministry experiment they have chosen. Just as they do in their vocational spheres, the group members will be actively paying attention, listening to the people they meet, listening to God, and listening to one another. They will reflect on their experiences with the ministry experiment in the reflection meetings as part of the process of discerning how God may be calling their church to join him in his mission.

PHASE 3: DECIDE ON A FINAL MINISTRY EXPERIMENT

It's great that the VCG participants have, by this point, learned a lot about their community and their places of vocation. It's great that they have gotten to know each other better. It's great that God has been at work in them, forming and shaping them, and deepening their faith.

But it can't stop there. Now the VCG participants have to *do* something with all that they have learned.

The final phase of the VCG process involves deciding on a final ministry experiment. The group has already conducted a small, simple ministry experiment. But now they need to try something bigger. Something that might feel a bit riskier. Something that could turn out to look like a wild success or a significant failure.

But it needs to be done. We are called to join God in what God is up to in the world. This final ministry experiment is our way of saying, "Okay, here is how we have seen God at work over the last year. Perhaps God is calling us to join in his mission by…."

My recommendation is to have an extended final reflection retreat where the group can take the time it needs to thoughtfully decide on a final ministry experiment.

Conduct a Final Reflection Retreat

After ten to twelve months of vocational engagement and reflection, the VCG participants are ready for the final reflection meeting. This final reflection meeting should be a half-day or full-day retreat in which the group reviews all that they have discovered over the course of the Vocational Connection Group process.

Back at the halfway point, after five or six months of meeting together, the VCG came up with a simple ministry experiment. They engaged in the ministry experiment and they reflected on it in the following months.

Now, with all that they have learned from a year of action-reflection, sharing, and prayer, the group is ready to dream up a final ministry experiment. This ministry experiment will be more fully-formed than the first one. In other words, whereas the first ministry experiment may have simply involved walking the neighborhood and praying for neighbors, the goal of this final ministry experiment will be to intentionally bless people and restore shalom. Here are a few examples:

- VCG members at a church in a college town may have sensed a need for connection among college students in their neighborhood and they want to experiment by setting up a free midnight hot dog stand on Friday nights where church members can connect with college students.
- Another church may have discovered a need for healthy adult presence in children's lives in their local schools, so they organize or volunteer for after-school tutoring.
- Still another church may have sensed a need for

men to embrace their roles as dads and husbands, so the men in the VCG start a weekly men's group at the local craft brewery to talk about issues around raising children and loving their spouses well.

Once they settle on a ministry to try, it is recommended that they continue to use the language of "experimentation." Why? Because there must be the freedom to fail. Calling it an experiment alerts the congregation that success is not guaranteed—and that that's okay. At the same time, calling it an experiment can sound very inviting. Who doesn't want to be a part of something new, even cutting edge?

Sample Agenda for Final Reflection Retreat

What should this final Reflection Retreat look like? Here's a sample agenda for a 5-hour Reflection Retreat:

9:00 – Gather (15 min.)
9:15 – Dwelling in Scripture (30 min.)
9:45 – Sharing Stories from the previous month (45 min.)
10:30 – Prayer (15 min.)
10:45 - Break (15 min.)
11:00 – Review and brainstorm primary themes that have emerged over the course of the year (60 min.)
12:00 – Lunch (45 min.)
12:45 – Imagine and plan a final ministry experiment (60 min.)
1:45 – Closing prayer (15 min.)
2:00 – Adjourn

It Doesn't End Here

Doing a Vocational Connection Group once will probably not be enough to truly transform a congregation. Transformation takes time. It is a process of learning, of listening, of experimentation, and of deepening individual church members' relationships with Jesus. It is also a process that opens us up to unexpected surprises. We can control our part in the VCG process, but we have no control over what God wants to do in us and through us. We may find at the end of the VCG process that God is not done with us yet. So, in order for a church to be positioned for deep transformation, the Vocational Connection Group process will likely need to be repeated again and again.

After the first Vocational Connection Group has finished its work, you should consider forming a new group. This new group will not only discover *new* ways that God is at work in their vocational spheres, but a new group will allow for more people from the congregation to get engaged in the process of intentionally connecting with their neighbors as the Body of Christ. A new VCG will help more people discover that God is already at work through them in ways they hadn't imagined. In other words, it allows more congregation members to experience this process of deep spiritual formation as they engage their vocational spheres and listen deeply to God and to one another.

Wouldn't it be amazing if—over time—half the congregation were to experience being part of a Vocational Connection Group? Or 75% of the congregation? Or even 100%? Imagine what God might do in a church where a majority of the congregation has intentionally entered their places of vocation, listened to their neighbors, listened to their fellow VCG participants, and listened to God! Imagine what God can do through a church like that!

AFTERWORD

"I wish I had been a pastor during the 1960's."

I literally had that exact thought several years ago. It was in one of those frustrating moments when I didn't know how to lead the church I was serving. I remember thinking about how easy it would have been to get people to show up on Sunday mornings back in those Christendom years. All you had to do is have good music and good preaching.[1]

Not that good music and good preaching aren't important. They can be a real blessing to people who come to worship. But the reality is that, in this Post-Christendom world, these are not enough to get people to show up on Sunday mornings.

And maybe getting people to show up on Sunday mornings is the wrong focus. Maybe we need to start thinking about "success" in new ways.

I am currently serving a small church in the farming community of Westmorland, California. Before becoming their interim pastor, I had been guest preaching there about once or twice a month. Occasionally, I would meet with their leadership team after church and offer some thoughts about mission and ministry. I asked them what their church did beyond Sunday morning services. How were they participating with God's work in the world the rest of the week?

They looked at each other, looked at me, and said, "Not much."

I guess those conversations got some wheels turning (at least, that's what they tell me), because a few months later, Westmorland Community Presbyterian Church opened a food pantry. While they did not go through a formal VCG process, they had spent enough time with people in their community to know that food insecurity is one of the biggest challenges in the town of Westmorland.[2]

Over the next few months, as people in the community learned about the new food pantry, WCPC began providing food to more and more individuals and families. Westmorland only has about 800 households. As of this writing, the WCPC food pantry serves over 100 of those 800 households!

Real people with real needs are experiencing some shalom in their lives because a few members of Westmorland Community Presbyterian Church listened to their neighbors, to one another, and to God. They asked, "How can we join God in the work that God is up to in this community?" And they implemented a ministry experiment —the food pantry.

Here is a church whose primary concern just a year or two ago revolved around how many people showed up on Sunday mornings. These days they celebrate every Sunday how many people were blessed because of the food pantry.

We live in a damaged and sin-scarred world. We live in a world in which shalom has been broken. It is a world that needs so desperately the life-giving love and healing of God. It is a world that needs the good news that God loves them so much that his Son, Jesus, came to live a life of shalom for us, die a death of shalom for us, and be raised to a new life of perfect shalom. It is because of the life, death, and resurrection of Jesus that restored shalom is not only possible, but promised.

We, the people of God, have been called to be the vessel of God's love and shalom. We have not been called to grow our attendance or our budgets. We have not been called to be the biggest or best church in town. We have been called to participate with God in the restoration of shalom.

May we take whatever steps are necessary to discern where and how God is already at work. May we leave behind any notions of worldly success and seek only to be the life-giving presence of Jesus in the world. May we listen to our neighbors, to each other, and to God so we might discern how God is calling us.

And as we live out our call to bring healing to the world, may we experience the love and shalom of God in our own lives and our own congregations.

ACKNOWLEDGMENTS

This book took me a long time to write. No, I take that back. The actual writing didn't take that long. It was all the stops and starts along the way. And so I'm grateful to all those who helped me keep going when I started getting tired.

The origin of this book goes back to my Doctor of Ministry program at Fuller Theological Seminary which I started in 2007. The instructors for my Missional Leadership cohort were Alan Roxburgh and Mark Lau Branson. Both of them opened my eyes to a whole new way of thinking about ministry. Several of my cohort-mates also stand out for me. Pete Seiferth, Steve Wilde, Jin Cho, and Mark Manassee helped me get clarity on what exactly my Neighborhood Connection Group experiment was meant to achieve.

After a painful departure from a former congregation, Geoff Hsu and Shauna Schneider invited me onto the staff of Flourish San Diego, an organization that exists to help churches and people participate in God's mission of restoring shalom in the world through our seemingly "ordinary" vocations. My time with Flourish was a time of great healing for me, as well as a time for me to get clarity on what really matters in ministry. It was at Flourish that I wrote most of Part 1 of this book. All of the Flourish staff played a significant part in my thinking, reflecting, and healing. Thank you to Geoff and Shauna, as well as Penny Leavitt, Josh Kerkhoff, Daniel So, and Cody Vermillion.

I did a lot of guest preaching while I was on staff with Flourish San Diego. On one such occasion, I met a sprightly woman named Kitty Bucholtz, who introduced herself as a writer. After a conversation or two, Kitty said, "I'd be willing to coach you in the writing process...for one dollar." I said, "Deal!" Kitty has been invaluable to me, both in the creative and technical aspects of getting this book finished. Oh, and Kitty... I still owe you a dollar.

These last few years of ministry have not been easy. There is no way I could have gotten through this season of my life if it weren't for my wife, Robin, and my three kids, Micah, Macy, and Drew. We've seen fire and we've seen rain. And we're looking forward to some sunny days—wouldn't it be nice if they'd never end? Thank you, Robin! And thank you, kids!

I'm also grateful to those who committed a year (okay, more like nine or ten months) of their lives to be a part of the original Neighborhood Connection Group experiment. I learned a lot through our conversations, our questions, and our prayers.

And, finally, I want to thank all of my beta readers—Jin Cho, Jason Coker, David Quel, Ron Musch, David Watson, Stasi McAteer, Gus Wright, Jackson Clelland, Jan Farley, Tiffany Hollums, Vince Larson, Geoff Hsu, and Jeya So. Some of you read part of the manuscript. Some of you read the whole thing. And all of you gave really valuable feedback. Thank you!

FOR MORE INFORMATION ABOUT:

- Vocational Connection Groups
- Spiritual Formation
- Healthy Church Leadership
- And more

Visit www.markuswatson.com

NOTES

Introduction

1. There's a tension here, isn't there? Numbers can be a very helpful diagnostic. Paying attention to attendance numbers and offerings and small group participation is important. But we can't let these numbers become idols. Perhaps there are other metrics we could learn to track. Is there some way to count the number of people in our city or community who were blessed because they experienced sacrificial kindness from our church members? Can we somehow track the degree to which people in our churches are drawing closer to Jesus? These are just as, if not more, important than the typical metrics of attendance and giving.

1. Coffee, Smog Checks, and Chuck E. Cheese

1. Cited in Maxwell, John C. *The 21 Indispensible Qualities of a Leader* (Nashville: Thomas Nelson, 1999), 130.
2. Myers, A. C. "Peace." In *The Eerdmans Bible Dictionary* (Grand Rapids: Eerdmans, 1987).
3. https://fhpc.org/preschool/
4. http://www.yaposhomecatering.com/

2. From Outcast to Overseer

1. Guder, Darrell. *Missional Church: A Vision for the Sending of the Church in North America* (Grand Rapids: Eerdmans, 1998), 5-6.
2. Bolsinger, Tod. *Canoeing the Mountains: Christian Leadership in Uncharted Territory* (Downers Grove: Intervarsity, 2015), 11.
3. Sweet, Leonard. *The Church in Emerging Culture: Five Perspectives* (Grand Rapids: Zondervan, 2003), 17.
4. Kreider, Alan. *The Change of Conversion and the Origin of Christendom* (Eugene: Wipf and Stock, 1999), 94.
5. To be clear, I will not be arguing that church attendance is unimportant or that we can fully live our faith apart from the Body of Christ. We are called to gather regularly to encourage one another,

strengthen one another, worship together, and receive God's Word. See Matthew 18:20, Acts 2:46-47, Hebrews 10:24-25.

6. Kreider, *The Change of Conversion and the Origin of Christendom*, 33.
7. Cultural and political powerlessness, that is. Spiritual power, on the other hand—and even moral authority—was something the church had in abundance.
8. Harvey, Barry A. *Another City* (Harrisburg: Trinity, 1999), 71.
9. Harvey, *Another City*, 81.
10. Harvey, *Another City*, 37.
11. Harvey, *Another City*, 67.
12. Harvey, *Another City*, 68.
13. Harvey, *Another City*, 95.
14. There were also eventually the monastics who didn't technically fit into the category of clergy. They were "ordinary" Christians who felt called to live lives of deep discipleship—which, in the pre-Christendom era, had been the norm for all Christians.
15. Kreider, *The Change of Conversion and the Origin of Christendom*, 96.
16. Lohfink, Gerhard. *Jesus and Community* (Philadelphia: Fortress, 1984), 132.
17. Kreider, *The Change of Conversion and the Origin of Christendom*, 98-99.
18. Infrequent church attendance, I would argue, is not inherently bad. I suspect there are many in the younger generations who simply are not interested in the mere doing of church stuff. They want to be a part of something bigger than themselves and may not be finding it in the local church—or at least not on Sunday mornings.

3. Luther's Milkmaid

1. Cited by Dan Doriani in a blog post titled, "The Power—and Danger —in Luther's Concept of Work," https://www.thegospelcoalition.org/article/the-power-and-danger-in-luthers-concept-of-work
2. The Westminster Shorter Catechism puts it like this:

   Q: What is the chief end of man?

   A: The chief end of man is to glorify God and enjoy him forever.

4. Finding Christ in the Situation

1. Newbigin, Lesslie. *The Open Secret,* rev. ed. (Grand Rapids: William B. Eerdmans, 1995), 56.
2. Newbigin, *The Open Secret*, 61.

3. Schreiter, Robert. *Constructing Local Theologies.* (Maryknoll: Orbis, 2002), 39.

5. Beyond Thingification

1. Schreiter, *Constructing Local Theologies*, 92.
2. Sedmak, Clemens. *Doing Local Theology: A Guide for Artisans of a New Humanity*. (Maryknoll: Orbis, 2002), 37.
3. Sedmak, *Doing Local Theology*, 14-15.
4. Sedmak, *Doing Local Theology*, vii.
5. Sedmak, *Doing Local Theology*, 147.
6. Sedmak, *Doing Local Theology*, 147.
7. Groome, Thomas H. *Sharing Faith: A Comprehensive Approach to Religious Education and Pastoral Ministry* (Eugene: Wipf and Stock, 1991), 331.
8. Groome, *Sharing Faith*, 331.
9. Schreiter, *Constructing Local Theologies*, 92.
10. Groome, *Sharing Faith*, 144.
11. Groome, *Sharing Faith*, 144.
12. Groome, *Sharing Faith*, 144.
13. Pascale, Richard T., Mark Milleman, and Linda Gioja, *Surfing the Edge of Chaos: The Laws of Nature and the New Laws of Business* (New York: Three Rivers, 2000), 202.
14. Pascale, *Surfing the Edge of Chaos*, 203.
15. Marquardt, Michael J. *Optimizing the Power of Action Learning: Real-Time Strategies for Developing Leaders, Building Teams, and Transforming Organizations*. (Boston: Davies Black, 2009), 71.
16. Block, Peter. *Community: The Structure of Belonging* (San Francisco: Berrett-Koehler, 2008), 103.
17. Marquardt, *Optimizing the Power of Action Learning*, 71.
18. Marquardt, *Optimizing the Power of Action Learning*, 74.
19. Palmer, Parker J. *To Know As We Are Known* (San Francisco: Harper San Francisco, 1993), 11.
20. Palmer, *To Know As We Are Known*, 11.
21. Block, *Community*, 33.
22. Block, *Community*, 33.
23. Marquardt, *Optimizing the Power of Action Learning*, 95.
24. Marquardt, *Optimizing the Power of Action Learning*, 96.
25. Marquardt, *Optimizing the Power of Action Learning*, 112.
26. Palmer, *To Know As We Are Known*, 71.
27. Palmer, *To Know As We Are Known*, 71.

6. Planning and Purpose

1. Marquardt, *Optimizing the Power of Action Learning*, 31.
2. Marquardt, *Optimizing the Power of Action Learning*, 31.

Afterword

1. I don't know if that's actually true, but that's what I imagine. No doubt ministry in the 1960's also had challenges.
2. Food insecurity is what happens when people run out of food before the next check arrives. There is a lot of poverty in Westmorland and a lot of families that have a hard time feeding their children through the entire month.

Made in the USA
San Bernardino, CA
14 March 2020